FLESH AND SPIRIT
CONFLICT

PREVIOUSLY PUBLISHED WITH RESOURCE PUBLICATIONS

Nonfiction

Storms Are Faith's Workout: Preparing Christians for Spiritual Ambush (2018).
Faith's Journey Confronts Obstacles: Instructing God's Soldiers to Overcome in His Armor (2019).
Satan's Strategy to Torment Through Physical Ambush: Educating God's Soldiers of Satan's Plot to Shatter Faith through Sickness and Disease (2019).
Spiritual Shipwreck on the Horizon: Exhorting Christians to Contend for the Faith and Comprehend the Deceitfulness of Sin (2019).
Satan Has No Authority Over God's Soldier: Illuminating Godlike Faith (2019).
God: The Holy Spirit: The Conquering Power Within (2019).
Signs of the Time: Warning: Lukewarm Christianity Accepts Deception (2020)

Fiction

The Elfdins and the Gold Temple: An Oralee Chronicle (2018).
Charlie McGee and the Leprechaun: Life's Curious Twist of Events (2019).
The Shrines of Manitoba: Dark Secrets Shall Be Brought to Light (2019).
Guilty As Blood: One Can Make a Difference (2019).
Back From the Dead: Light Shines As the Noonday Sun (2020).

FLESH AND SPIRIT CONFLICT

The Inner Battle of Choice

R. C. JETTE

RESOURCE *Publications* · Eugene, Oregon

FLESH AND SPIRIT CONFLICT
The Inner Battle of Choice

All Scriptures are taken from the KING JAMES VERSION (KJV): KING
JAMES VERSION, public domain.

Resource Publications
An Imprint of Wipf and Stock Publishers
199 W. 8th Ave., Suite 3
Eugene, OR 97401

www.wipfandstock.com

PAPERBACK ISBN: 978-1-7252-6912-5
HARDCOVER ISBN: 978-1-7252-6911-8
EBOOK ISBN: 978-1-7252-6913-2

Manufactured in the U.S.A.   04/21/20

This book is dedicated to my Lord Jesus Christ who makes all things possible by faith!

Also, to my husband, Paul, who has been a continued source of encouragement to me.

I want to mention my son PJ, my daughters Dawn, and Christina. My grandsons, Andrew, Matthew, Joshua, granddaughter Keira. A special thanks to Susanna and Mike.

To my mother Rita Christina, my sister Carol Ann, my brother Frank Herbert, my brother Raymond Griffin, and my granddaughter, Sarah Elizabeth, I miss you all and await our grand reunion day.

My heartfelt thanks is given to Wipf and Stock Publishers for their continued publication of my books under their Resource Publications. I thank their staff who have constantly made this challenge more tolerable. Special thanks is given to Matthew Wimer, George Callihan, Shannon Carter, and Savanah Landerholm to whom words cannot convey my gratitude.

And he was withdrawn from them about a stone's cast, and kneeled down, and prayed, Saying, Father, if thou be willing, remove this cup from me: nevertheless not my will, but thine, be done. And there appeared an angel unto him from heaven, strengthening him. And being in agony he prayed more earnestly: and his sweat was as it were great drops of blood falling down to the ground.

LUKE 22:41–44

Contents

Introduction

ALTHOUGH THIS BOOK WILL educate us in realizing the battle raging within because of our free-will, it is meant to unfold how to overcome the battle to make the right choice. All our decisions or choices, as God's soldiers, should give glory to God. Each chapter will build on the previous to help give us an understanding of how the inner battle rages. When I say build upon the previous, it means that each chapter will help illuminate the conflict of flesh and Spirit and the inner battle or turmoil to help us make the choice that glorifies God.

Once we begin to understand different aspects of what happens between our flesh and Spirit, we'll gain wisdom to put our flesh under and yield to the Spirit.

As I was meditating upon Galatians 5:17, I was seeking the Lord as to why so many Christians are making compromising and wrong choices in their life. He reminded me of the battles in my life that I've had to overcome in order to choose his will and not mine. Making the right choice between faith and unbelief takes an incredible determination to deny self what it wants. Sometimes, it's most agonizing. However, we must decide if we are for God or self. No one else can make that choice for us. It has to be a commitment to God based on a love that's deep rooted in our being.

We tend to forget that we're in a war with an unrelenting enemy who works overtime to get us to yield to our flesh and not the Spirit. We face a supernatural enemy who is unyielding in his vendetta to destroy our faith. It's our choice, our free-will, our love of God, and our belief in his love for us that determines if the enemy succeeds.

This is easily seen in the garden where Eve allowed her flesh to be so enticed that she sinned against the commandment of God. I will expose this more clearly in chapter 5 revealing the effects of choice.

This book is meant to instruct us and disclose how to truly overcome our inner battle and choose what's right in God's eyes. Knowledge is the key to winning the conflict between the flesh and the Spirit and overcome to the glory of God.

As I've stated in my other books, there seems to be much ignorance in the church. A lack of knowledge leads to defeat. Let me explain, if the enemy is planning an attack and there's no proper intelligence given, disaster results. This is clearly seen in the natural, if our armed forces don't have proper intelligence, it could be catastrophic. In the spiritual, our proper intelligence is God's word and being sensitive to the prompting of the Holy Spirit who enables us to be aware and not ignorant of Satan's devices (2 Corinthians 2:11).

This life is full of storms, obstacles, demonic strategies, Goliaths, etc. Unless we learn how to win the battle raging within between our flesh and Spirit, we will be overcome by Satan's tactics. He is working overtime to get us to complain, to murmur, to grow weary, to give up on God, and to destroy our faith.

My prayer for you who have picked up this book is that you will be inspired with the truth to live a victorious life, understand the consequences of yielding to the flesh, and choose to be for God and not against him. Whenever we choose flesh, we have chosen to be against God.

Listen to me, you have the power living within you to overcome this battle, this Goliath, this storm, this obstacle. The Holy Spirit of God, who is the conquering power within, has armed you with all you need to win each and every battle. Please don't be discouraged, but read each chapter and finish this book. Allow the Holy Spirit to encourage you and to build you up in the faith. You are MORE than a conqueror through him that loves you (Romans 8:37). With Christ, you can make it through this storm. You can defeat this Goliath trying to take you down. You can overcome this obstacle. You are the child of the God of the Universe who speaks worlds into existence, who forgives all sins, who heals all sickness and disease, and who will supply all your needs. There is NOTHING that He can't do if you believe (Mark 9:23).

Soldier put on your whole armor of God and listen to the Holy Spirit as you read through the pages. Through them, you should understand how to overcome the conflict of flesh and spirit, win the inner battle of choice for the glory of God, and hear, "Well done, thou good and faithful servant!"

Chapter 1

Pricks in Your Eyes

But if ye will not drive out the inhabitants of the land from before you; then it shall come to pass, that those which ye let remain of them shall be *pricks* in your eyes, and thorns in your sides, and shall vex you in the land wherein ye dwell. Moreover, it shall come to pass, that I shall do unto you, as I thought to do unto them.

Numbers 33:55–56

God wants his people delivered from whatever could hinder our living above the influence or control of sin. Yet, many are living in the wilderness of defeat and never enter into the Promise Land.

It's imperative to understand this book's intention is to help us comprehend the entanglement of sin and its consequences in our life. Sin (unbelief) will keep us in the wasteland of defeat and not living in the freedom from sin Christ gave us (John 8:36).

Let me explain why all sin is unbelief. Unbelief doesn't believe that Christ has given us power over sin. Instead, we yield to the desire of the flesh. Our flesh was born in sin, and it craves the lust of the flesh, the lust of the eyes, and the pride of life.

Unless we overcome the inner battle of choice between our flesh and Spirit to the glory of God, sin will result. With sin, there will be negative, adverse, harmful, and destructive effects in our life.

> But thou shalt utterly destroy them; namely, the Hittites, and the Amorites, the Canaanites, and the Perizzites, the Hivites, and the Jebusites; as the Lord thy God hath commanded thee: that they teach you not to do after all their abominations, which they have done unto their gods; so should ye sin against the Lord your God (Deuteronomy 20:17–18).

What I want us to comprehend is that when we were born again, we, as Israel, had a mighty deliverance out of bondage. But that is not all the Holy Spirit wants to deliver us from. In the wilderness, we need to trust God to supply our needs. We may be delivered from Egypt or the world, but do our actions, our thoughts, etc. reveal that we have learned to deny self? Do we lack love, obedience, worship to God? Are we constantly complaining and missing the things of the world? Whenever there's a constant desire for worldly things, it's clear that self rules and not God.

If we don't learn to have faith in God, we'll wander in the wilderness like the Israelites until we die. If we learn to have faith in God, we'll be like Joshua and Caleb who enter into the Promise Land.

This is where many of us get it wrong. We think that once we're out of the wilderness and in the Promise Land that life should be a piece of cake. What we don't realize is that the Promise Land is full of enemies. The Canaanites, the Jebusites, the Hivites, the Hittites, the Amorites, and the Perizzites who must be conquered before the fullness of the Promise Land can be enjoyed.

Who are the Canaanites to God's soldiers? They are not only worldly persecution, but the old nature (our flesh), the lust of the flesh, the lust of the eyes, the pride of life, and the works of the flesh.

Unless we conquer self, our old nature, fleshly appetites, etc., we'll never conquer the anti-God persecution around us, nor will we fully enjoy God's promises. In order to be an inhabitant of the Promise Land, we need self-deliverance.

Let me explain. Many of God's soldiers have entered the Promise Land. That means we've been delivered from the bondage of sin, have come through the wilderness learning to trust God. However, time has caused us to have one foot in the Promise Land and one foot in some bondage we were delivered from. Or we miss the leaks and onions of the world. In other words, we find denying self too much. When this happens, we start on the road to self-indulgence, or the wide and broad path to destruction.

We, as Israel, allow the Canaanites to keep their high places. Instead of completely destroying the enemies (our old nature), we allow them to remain. Before long, they have taken back the land (our life). We start to compromise God's word to satisfy our flesh. We allow a little leaven of the world to corrupt. If we don't nip it in the bud, we'll be thoroughly leavened by what the flesh wants and not what God wants.

We have to understand that the world around us entices our fleshly appetites, and we yield to it. I explained how we can start to go back by thinking this isn't too bad or that's not too bad in my book, *Storms Are Faith's Workout*.

Anyway, when we are lukewarm, we complain about not enjoying God's promises. We are in that condition because we refuse to deny self and conquer the self-Canaanites that are the lust of the flesh, the lust of the eyes, and the pride of life.

> And he said to them all, If any man will come after me, let him deny himself, and take up his cross daily, and follow me (Luke 9:23).

In the above Scripture, Jesus gave the secret or the key to self-deliverance. The only way for us to follow Jesus is to deny self on a daily basis. If we are indulging our flesh (self) we are not following Jesus. We can't claim to be a follower of Jesus Christ when we give into our flesh and obey it. We can only follow Jesus as we deny self and take up our cross daily.

If we don't conquer, overcome, subjugate self, we just stumble around the Promise Land without any of its goodness flowing with milk and honey. The Holy Spirit has been trying to reveal the importance of self-denial in order to possess the Promise Land. Not until we have done as Joshua and Caleb, have been delivered from self, understand the necessity for self-deliverance, and mastered its denial, do we enjoy the land of promise.

How I see it is that we are on the threshold of the Promise Land and all the Canaanites, all the enemies that want to keep us from our rightful inheritance are lined up and fighting with all they have to keep us in sin, sickness, lacking, complaining, etc.

Listen to me, they have been keeping God's soldiers from enjoying the promises and blessings of God for century upon century. They know how to keep Christians from taking what God has given us through enticing us to compromise or give into our flesh. We fight the battle for a little while and then grow weary in the well-doing and never reap God's promise because we give into the flesh.

Warfare is hard. It's an arduous, laborious, and strenuous endeavor. To win the battle over all the Canaanites (self and worldly persecution) is difficult to accomplish. We will never win over these enemies in the world, unless we have first won the battle over self. Once self is put under subjection to the will of God, the spiritual warfare against the Canaanites becomes less of a struggle. If self has been crucified with Christ, the inner battle of choice is quickly won.

If these enemies inspired by Satan can't get us to be discouraged, to doubt, to grow weary, to be jealous, to complain, etc. in the battle, we win. Why? Because Jesus already won it.

When we finally learn to put on the whole armor of God, take the shield of faith, the sword of the Spirit, which is the word of God, we stand in the power and might of God. When the devil sees that, he knows he can't play his trickery or his lies on us, and he flees (James 4:7).

Let's look at our opening Scriptures for this chapter to gain a better understanding. If we don't drive the Canaanites out of our life, they will overtake us. What is this saying? It's revealing to us that as we gain ground, we must make sure that we destroy the previous inhabitants. All sin must be annihilated. In other words, if we don't conquer the sin that has been revealed to us, it will eventually consume us. We must not compromise with our flesh and think it's not that bad, other Christians are indulging in much worse, God wants us happy, etc. Thoughts like that are fleshly led. God never compromises his word and wants us to be uncompromising also.

Let's take the teaching of these Scriptures further. If we don't stand against the sin of the world around us, God will allow the evil of the world to trample us. God promises in the verses in Numbers that if we don't stand against the evil inhabitants, He will do to us what He had thought to do to them. This is a very sobering promise and should help us to silence the inner battle of choice when the conflict of flesh and Spirit is raging. Yet, how many still yield to the flesh and find ourselves in a calamity because we chose to ignore God's word, our own conscience, and the prompting of the Holy Spirit?

We have not been denying sin in our life, and we have not been standing against sin in our Nation. If we were, there would not be such a rise in socialism, Muslims in our government, murder of our unborn and full-term children, legalizing homosexual marriage, etc.

Soldier of God, it's time to conquer our flesh, and win the battle of choice in favor of God and his will. The Canaanites (our flesh, the world, Satan, and whatever is contrary to God's word) has no power or authority over us. God gave us (his children) the legal authority to overcome any Satanic storm, obstacle, strategy, etc.

> And he answering said, Thou shalt love the Lord thy God with all thy heart, and with all thy strength, and with all thy mind. . . (Luke 10:27).

It's time to be delivered from the pricks in our eyes. Let me help us to understand this. The BBC did a film about the Snow Queen by Hans Christian Anderson. In it Gerda and her mother take in a beggar boy named Kay. One winter night a piece of glass (from the evil Snow Queen's mirror) pierces Kay's eye. After that, his heart becomes cold making him angry and unhappy. He was overcome by the seduction of the Snow Queen.

She takes him to her palace in the frozen north. Through faith, love, and courage, Gerda decides that she must find him and begins a perilous quest through strange lands. When she faces the

Snow Queen, she is told that she has a power greater than the Snow Queen's, because Gerda's power comes from her heart.

What I'm endeavoring to show is that we can be easily pricked in our eyes by our flesh to yield to its lust and the evil around us. However, love is the most powerful factor in the Universe. God sending his Son to die was out of his great love for us. Christ's self-sacrifice for us was the result of a love that we can't comprehend. Our love for the Lord will enable us to be delivered from self, the enticement of the Canaanites, and keep pricks from getting into our eyes!

Chapter 2

Who's Your Confidence

Trust in the Lord with all thine heart; and lean
not unto thine own understanding. In all thy ways
acknowledge him, and he shall direct thy paths.

PROVERBS 3:5–6

TO TRUST IN MEANS to be confident in; to be secure without fear.
Therefore to have confidence is the state of feeling certain about the
truth of something. It's being assured or certain about something
or someone.

If we trust the Lord, we will not lean unto our own understanding. That means we don't lean to or toward what we think, our
understanding, our education, our logic, etc. We don't lean on our
perception or how we see things. The Hebrew word is translated as
not to support one's self. In other words, we are not to lean on self, not
to rely on self, not to rest on self, and not to have confidence in self.

> For thou hast trusted in thy wickedness: tho hast said,
> None seeth me. Thy wisdom and thy knowledge, it hath
> perverted thee. . .(Isaiah 47:10).

Our wisdom and our knowledge, that comes from man, has warped the thinking of God's soldiers who lean unto our own understanding. Using the wisdom and knowledge of man causes us to put our trust in self or man and turn us away from God's way.

Let me make something clear. If we place our all in his will, it isn't going to be easy on our flesh. Many times what we want is not God's will for our life. We can be deceived into thinking something is of God, when it's the opposite of what God wants or wills. Learning to overcome the inner battle of choice between the flesh and the Spirit is to choose God's way. As we go along in this book, things will unfold more clearly.

Proverbs 3:5–6 is not only a promise but a warning. The *promise* is if our heart is fixed on God, He IS the one guiding our paths. When we acknowledge God in all we do, we can be assured of his guidance. The *warning* is if we are not trusting God with all our heart, are leaning unto our own understanding, and don't acknowledge him in all our ways, He is NOT directing our paths.

God's soldiers must comprehend the biggest or one of the biggest problems in the church is the referring our ways to self. In other words, we are being self-supportive. This is being directed and supported by self or our flesh. It's being directed by what we want or desire and not what God wants or desires. Whenever we lean on our own understanding (our fleshly knowledge), we lean on self. This is man's wisdom, logic, education, or comprehension. Anything to do with man is the flesh, the carnal nature, the old nature, or the fallen nature.

We become discontent in God's way, and we begin to seek our own way. God's soldiers must stop leaning on logic or our own desires, and make sure we're leaning on God's way or doing his will. In other words, how many times do we ignore the inner battle and move on impulse or self-desire? We pay no heed to the Spirit trying to warn us. Instead, we give into our flesh, and disregard the Holy Spirit's prompting us to be quiet, don't go there, don't do that, go there, do that, etc. Only being led by the Holy Spirit will enable us to make the right choice.

Let's understand what this is teaching. If the Spirit is directing, we will make the right choice. If our flesh is directing, we will make the wrong choice. There is no way our flesh can make the right choice or do that which is pleasing in God's sight.

> Enter ye in at the straight gate: for wide is the gate, and broad is the way, that leadeth to destruction, and many there be which go in thereat. Because straight is the gate and narrow is the way, which leadeth unto life, and few there be that find it (Matthew 7:13–14).

The path directed by God is very narrow, confined, restricted, etc. to the flesh. It squeezes the flesh and makes it uneasy. The flesh doesn't want to be constricted, constrained, or limited. It wants to be free to indulge in the lust of the flesh, the lust of the eyes, and the pride of life without any limitations. In other words, the flesh fellowships with the Canaanites.

Why does leaning unto our understanding or what we think turn us away from God's way? Because God's thoughts are not our thoughts, neither are our ways his ways. For as the heavens are higher than the earth, so are God's ways higher than our ways, and his thoughts than our thoughts (Isaiah 55:8–9). No matter how right the way may seem to us, if it's not God's way, it will lead to death (Proverbs 14:12).

In what manner can we acknowledge God in all our ways, in all our life, in all our conduct? We do it by placing every aspect of our life (our thoughts, what we do, where we live, where we work, etc.) in his will.

The gauge I use to help Christians in learning to discern God's voice when I'm asked, "How can we know if it's God's will?" I teach this simple indicator. I tell them if it's comfortable for us (easy on our flesh), we can be 99 percent sure, it's not God's will. On the other hand, if it's uncomfortable for us (difficult on our flesh), we can be 99 percent sure, it's God's will. Once we learn that God's will is contrary to what our flesh wants, we start to hear his voice over the voice of self. Because we've learned to deny self, we conquer the inner battle between flesh and Spirit and yield to the Spirit.

Because we'll never, in our flesh, find the straight and narrow path to life, hearing his voice takes time and a constant choice of denying self (our flesh). In other words, if we continue to yield to our flesh, we'll never learn to discern the voice of God. Only comprehending that God's will is uncomfortable on our fleshly desires will we choose to deny self.

Let me give a simple example. We have diabetes and ask God if we can have that huge piece of chocolate cake. We believe we heard, "yes." Well, God would never tell us to do what could cause us to have too much sugar in our bodies that could lead to heart disease, stroke, kidney disease, etc. God's voice will always lead us to the straight and narrow path that will restrain, restrict, limit our flesh and help us destroy the Canaanites of the lust of the flesh, the lust of the eyes, and the pride of life..

> Not that I speak in respect of want: for I have learned in whatsoever state I am, therewith to be content (Philippians 4:11).

The Apostle Paul knew the key to being in God's will is to be uncomfortable in the flesh. It wasn't that he wouldn't have wanted something different, but he had learned to crucify his flesh and its wants of comfort outside of the narrow path. He understood the flesh and Spirit conflict and knew how to win the inner battle of choice.

The apostle was, in fact, claiming that he didn't care how difficult it was on his flesh, because it's God's will. He was willing to have his flesh squeezed, to have it uncomfortable. The discomfort in his flesh meant that if he lacked fleshly comforts, he was giving glory to him who gave himself to be squeezed, to be uncomfortable in his flesh to save us.

Only God can direct us or make straight our paths. The devil knows this. That's why he tries to get us to concentrate or acknowledge the storm, the obstacle, the strategy, the giant that squeezes and agonizes our flesh. When that happens, we begin to lean upon our own understanding and talk ourselves out of God's will into the will of the devil.

As I stated earlier, there is a way which seems right unto man, but the end thereof are the ways of death. Listen up. The way seems right to man. That means we can convince ourselves that it's right, but it will lead us out of God's will and place us on the wide road to Hell.

My people are destroyed for lack of knowledge (Hosea 4:6).

The prophet is referring to God's knowledge. Because God's soldiers lack a knowledge of God and his word, we are being destroyed. We must comprehend that man's knowledge, man's wisdom, man's understanding, or leaning on self is destroying God's people. It's leading many down or to the wide and broad gate to destruction.

> Study to shew thyself approved unto God, a workman that needeth not to be ashamed, rightly dividing the word of truth (2 Timothy 2:15).

Instead of studying God's word to get a knowledge of God, many of God's soldiers are listening to people who are not rightly dividing the Scriptures. Because their parent, pastor, teacher, etc. told them something, they take it as set in stone. They become adamant in what they've heard and never search the Scriptures to verify its truth.

We will not be judged by what someone taught us, but by what God's word says. Jesus made this clear in John 12:48 where He stated his word shall judge us. In other words, we can't use the excuse that's what so-and-so taught us. We are told to study to shew ourselves approved unto God. We answer for ourselves. We alone make our choices. What we choose to do is the result of our choice.

In order to have a knowledge of God, we must know his word. Without a knowledge of him, we will never trust him, confide in him, or love him with our whole being. Let's face it, how can we trust someone with our life, if we don't know him?

The devil spends more time, I believe, in deterring God's people from reading and studying their Bible. He knows a proper knowledge of God's word gives a proper understanding of God, and a proper understanding of God causes us to love him with all our heart. When we love the Lord with all our heart, we will then trust him with all our heart.

Let me explain, the degree in which we trust God is proportioned to our love for God. We can only trust someone in whom we love more than self.

As we comprehend that truth, we are prepared to deny our flesh, yield to the Spirit, and the inner battle of choice becomes easier. Because we love God, our confidence in his love to do what's best for us, enables us to deny self and make the choice for his will!

Chapter 3

Gratitude Equals Obligation

> For I am the least of the apostles, that am not meet to be called
> an apostle, because I persecuted the church of God. But by the
> grace of God, I am what I am: and his grace which was bestowed
> upon me was not in vain; but I labored more abundantly than
> they all: yet not I, but the grace of God which was with me.
>
> 1 CORINTHIANS 15:9–10

THIS CHAPTER WILL HELP us to see what we owe Christ. Our gratitude should cause a deep obligation to love and please him. Once
we get that truth deep into our heart, it will be an incredible help
for us to overcome the flesh and Spirit conflict and make the correct
inner choice.

In the above verse, the Apostle Paul refers to himself as *the
least of the apostles*. Yet, as we read the New Testament, we see he
wrote thirteen of the twenty-seven books. It's fourteen to us who
include him as the author of Hebrews. Anyway, he certainly wasn't
the least in humility, gifts, or labor.

According to 2 Corinthians 11:23–27, the apostle has quite a
resume of suffering for Christ. Five times he received thirty-nine

stripes from the Jews, was beaten three times with rods, was ship-wrecked, and a night and a day was in the deep. He found himself in journeyings often, in perils of waters, in perils of robbers, in perils by his countrymen, in perils by heathen, in perils in the city, in perils in the wilderness, in perils in the sea, in perils among false brethren, in weariness and painfulness, in hunger and thirst, in cold and nakedness.

> From henceforth let no man trouble me: for I bear in my body the marks of the Lord Jesus (Galatians 6:17).

He had the proof of his service physically. That means, it's quite incredible what the apostle had suffered for Christ's name's sake (Acts 9:16). Yet, he penned fourteen books encouraging us in our faith journey.

Think about it. He goes through all he suffered and claims, *"I am the least of the Apostles."* How can the greatest of the apostles in accomplishments for Christ claim to be the least or nothing in the Kingdom of God?

Listen to me, he wasn't trying to sound humble. There was no pretense on his part. He believed with all his heart that he was truly the least of God's ministers.

In order to help us to comprehend how Paul thought or how he saw things, we'll look at another Scripture text.

> But which of you, having a servant plowing or feeding cattle, will say unto him by and by, when he is come from the field, Go and sit down to meat? And will not rather say unto him, Make ready wherewith I may sup, and gird thyself, and serve me, till I have eaten and drunken; and afterward thou shalt eat and drink? Doth he thank that servant because he did the things that were commanded him? I trow not. So likewise ye, when ye shall have done all those things which are commanded you, say, We are unprofitable servants: we have done that which was our duty to do (Luke 17:7–10).

What those verses are revealing to us is that Paul knew no matter what he did in complete obedience to the word of God, he did nothing more than his duty. He understood whatever he did was the least he could do. Paul knew what he owed Christ and was willing to suffer whatever to win the prize of the high calling in Christ (Philippians 3:8–14).

Let's consider all that the apostle did in the call of duty and all he fulfilled. Yet, he considered himself to be nothing or the least of God's chosen.

How many of God's soldiers today spend more time bickering and complaining about our duty? Then when we perform some menial task, think within ourselves how much we've done for the Kingdom of God. We may claim to be nothing, but our hearts are puffed up with what we've done. If we do something for others, we go around and tell how much we've done for them.

Nowhere in the Scriptures can we find Jesus bragging about his sufferings for us. He did what He did out of love. When we truly love the Lord with our whole being, we do our duty out of love for him. That's exactly what Paul did.

When we think of the apostle's sufferings, we are reminded of Job and his sufferings. However, in this life, Paul's distresses never ceased as Job's did.

Think about that. He suffered week after week, month after month, year after year for Christ and the gospel, yet, Paul considered it his duty and expected no special adoration or applause.

Let's go deeper in, so to speak, to see more of what was in Paul's heart.

> There was a certain creditor which had two debtors: the one owed five hundred pence, and other fifty. And when they had nothing to pay, he frankly forgave them both. Tell me therefore, which of them will love him most? Simon answered and said, I suppose that he, to whom he forgave most. And he said unto him, Thou hast rightly judged. And he turned to the woman, and said unto Simon, Seest thou this woman? I entered into thine house, thou gavest me no water for my feet: but she hath washed my feet with tears, and wiped them with the hairs of her head. Thou gavest me no kiss: but this woman since the time I came in hath not ceased to kiss my feet. My head with oil thou didst not anoint: but this woman hath anointed my feet with ointment. Wherefore

I say unto thee, Her sins, which are many, are forgiven; for she loved much: but to whom little is forgiven, the same loveth little (Luke 7:41–47).

The crux of the above verses is Jesus states the one forgiven for a *very large* debt is largely grateful. Whereas, the one forgiven for a little debt is not very grateful.

That tells us the one forgiven for much is so grateful that his/her love for the one who forgave is a very deep love. The one forgiven for little is not very grateful and his/her love for the one who forgave is a little love.

Now, let's look back at our beginning Scripture text in 1 Corinthians 15:9–10. In those verses, Paul claims to be the least of the apostles because he persecuted the church. He sees his debt as so large that no one was worse than him. Then he goes on to say, *"But by the grace of God, I am what I am: and his grace which was bestowed upon me was not in vain: but I labored more abundantly than they all: yet not I, but the grace of God which was with me."* What a great love Paul had for Jesus. He knew the debt he owed, but could never pay.

He says that by the grace of God, I am what I am. In other words, by the free love and goodness of God, I who was before a blasphemer, a persecutor, and injurious have obtained mercy. I have never merited his love. Yet, his grace in me hath produced some fruit and his grace has not been wholly in vain.

In other words, How can I not love him and do all He asks of me without complaining when I'm reminded daily of what I did against him. Any fruit in my life is not because of me. That, too, I owe him; for it's his grace in me that has enabled me to do it.

Now, if we are born again, what is the degree of our gratitude? Do we believe we are obligated to the Lord? Do we comprehend we deserve to go to Hell? Do we believe because we are now a child of God, He owes us? What is our mindset?

I don't know how many times, I've been bewildered by Christians claiming this sin or that sin deserves to go to Hell. Yet, don't believe any sin committed by them was grounds to go to Hell.

We sing the song, *"He paid a debt He did not owe, I owed a debt I could not pay. I needed someone to wash my sins away. And now I sing a brand new song. Amazing Grace. Christ Jesus paid the debt that I could NEVER pay."*

If we truly recognize the debt is so large that we can *never* pay it, how can we not comprehend grace wipes out the debt that would have sent us to Hell? Do we truly comprehend that our debt is *too large* for us to even grasp its vastness? Do we realize what we owe Jesus for paying our debt? Do we grasp the fact that if He hadn't paid it, we'd be going to Hell? Do we understand that no matter what we do for the Lord isn't even a drop in the bucket?

Once that reality becomes a revelation, it causes a great love to swell up inside for Jesus. This love causes such a gratitude to the Lord that we feel obligated to do whatever it takes to deny ourselves and choose his will. Simply put, love for Christ will overpower our flesh, help us quench the inner battle, enable us to yield to the Spirit, and make the choice that gives glory to God!

Chapter 4

Faith vs. Unbelief

And the same day, when the even was come, He saith unto them,
Let us pass over unto the other side. And when they had sent away
the multitude, they took him even as he was in the ship. And there
were also with him other little ships. And there arose a great storm
of wind, And the waves beat into the ship, so that it was now full.
And He was in the hinder part of the ship, asleep on a pillow: And
they awake him, and say unto him, Master, carest thou not that we
perish? And He arose and rebuked the wind, and said unto the sea,
Peace, be still. And the wind ceased, and there was a great calm. And
he said unto them, Why are ye so fearful? How is it that ye have no
faith? And they feared exceedingly, and said one to another, What
manner of man is this, that even the wind and sea obey him?

MARK 4:35–41

WHEN IN GOD'S WILL expect to face storms, obstacles, and strategies of Satan. We need to learn from the faith of Jesus. Faith rests (is
at peace) during the trial. Faith realizes the reality is God's promises

and not the storm, or trial. Unbelief looks at the storm and over-looks or forgets the promises.

The Scriptures in Mark are a well-used sermon text. Although we are familiar with a Bible text doesn't mean we've gleaned all its nuggets. Sometimes a little twist in a known Scripture can bring forth a deeper revelation.

I know that the text in Mark was the foundation or nucleus for my book, *Storms Are Faith's Workout: Preparing Christians for Spiritual Ambush*. However, for this book, it will help us understand the conflict between our flesh and Spirit, our need to overcome the inner battle by choice, and by faith make the choice that glorifies God.

In Mark, it's obvious it was night time when Jesus commanded that He and the disciples pass over the sea from Galilee to the re-gion of the Gadarenes. Now, mind you, it had been a long day of teaching, and as a man, Jesus experienced the human weakness of fatigue. Thus, He was weary and fell asleep.

Before I continue, I want to bring forth an important fact that can't be overstressed. Never forget that Jesus was a man susceptible to all our human frailties and temptations. Yes, He was the God-man, but He emptied himself not of his divine nature, but his divine attributes or his ability to do miracles as God (Philippians 2:6–8). All that Christ did here was done as a man being led by the power and anointing of the Holy Spirit (Matthew 4:1–11).

We all know what happened after they were in the boat and heading for the region of the Gadarenes. They started out on a calm sea, but a sudden storm arose. The ship became full of water and the disciples feared for their lives. They certainly didn't appear to be men of faith during the storm.

I want us to think about that. How do we appear when we are in a severe storm or trial? Do people see us as God's soldiers of faith, or do they see us as fleshly people of unbelief? What kind of God do we portray during storms, facing mountainous obstacles, or combating Satan's strategies against our body? It's all based on the flesh and Spirit conflict, and which one we yield to during the inner battle of choice.

Okay, we see the disciples' unbelief caused them to accuse Jesus of not caring, "Carest thou not that we perish?" They believed that if Jesus cared, He wouldn't be sleeping. In other words, how can He care if He's sleeping when we are about to be destroyed or killed?

Of course, Jesus gets up and says, "Peace be still." He commanded the storm to be dumb, silent, or quiet. As soon as the storm is calmed, He immediately reprimands his disciples for their unbelief.

Let's look at the difference between faith and unbelief. Jesus is the example of faith. He is asleep or in perfect peace while the storm is raging. The disciples are the example of unbelief. They are frantic, overwhelmed by fear while the storm is raging.

The definition of faith is complete trust, complete confidence, firm or steadfast belief. Whereas, unbelief is lack of belief, lack of trust, lack of confidence, pliable or vacillating belief.

In other words, faith is firm and can't be moved. It's solid, steadfast. It never gives up, and it never surrenders. Whereas, unbelief is pliable, changes to whatever way the wind blows. It's fickle and unsteady.

Unbelief only sees what it experiences. It feels the boat rocking, sees the waves filling the boat, and the sea threatening them with death. We must understand that unbelief focuses on what it's experiencing, what it's suffering, what it's encountering, what it's feeling. It views only the natural realm of feelings, and focuses on its fears, worries, pain, finances, etc. Unbelief ONLY sees the storm.

On the other hand, faith doesn't see the experience, ignores its feelings, and focuses on the promises of God. Instead of looking at the boat full of water or the raging storm, faith sees the power and grace of God to give a peace that passes all understanding during the storm.

> Now faith is the substance of things hoped for, the evidence of things not seen (Hebrews 11:1).

The great characteristic and power of faith is to see what is NOT visible. Faith doesn't look at what it sees in the natural realm, because faith knows it's a lie. Why is the natural usually a lie? Because it's contrary to the promise of God. Faith knows the storm/trial is the opposite of the promise.

Faith doesn't look at the storm, it trusts in God's promises. Faith doesn't wonder or think God can do something. Faith KNOWS that with God nothing shall be impossible (Luke 1:37).

Okay, what does this have to do with our Scripture text in Mark? It has everything to do with it. Jesus said, "Let us pass over unto the other side." This is a command, a commission, a *promise*. He didn't say "Let us try to pass." He said, "Let us pass."

Now, if Christ said that we are to pass over, we will pass over. If God promises something, He is going to complete it. He cannot lie (Titus 1:2).

Please note, if and when God tells us to do something or promises us something, a sudden storm will appear. In my book, *Storms Are Faith's Workout*, I revealed this in detail. At present, we must know for a fact that a sudden storm will come. Whatever form it takes, whether opposition, discouragement, worry, anxiety, etc., it will feel like all Hell is coming against us.

Unless we understand this, we will never understand the flesh and Spirit conflict or how to overcome the inner battle to make the right choice.

To help us understand the difference between faith and unbelief, I want to interject something from my book about Godlike faith, *Satan Has No Authority Over God's Soldier: Illuminating Godlike Faith*. It's something that happened to me many years ago. There was this situation, and I was overwhelmed. As I was praying, I had a vision of being in the middle of an ocean, and I couldn't see land. I went to stand up and couldn't find the bottom. When I came back up, I cried, "Lord help me! I can't swim. I can't see any land." As I'm frantic in the water trying to stay up, the Lord said, "Be still, take deep breaths, be calm. Now, lay back, let the water hold you. Close your eyes, rest, and the current will take you to land."

As I did that, Scripture promises flooded my mind (Philippians 4:6–7; Isaiah 26:3; 1 John 4:18; John 4:18). Then I went from the vision to me in prayer and I jumped up and said, "Lord, I get it. I understand that Godlike faith sleeps during the storm and has perfect peace, because it trusts God. Faith doesn't dwell on the storm.

It looks beyond to God who is able to calm the storm. It's like Peter who walked on the water until he took his eyes from Christ to the storm. Whenever we take our eyes off Jesus, we'll sink.

Let me add to that story by revealing that God is able to calm the raging storm within us with a peace that passes all understanding and keep our hearts and minds through Christ Jesus (Philippians 4:6–7). That's why Jesus was able to sleep during the storm. He was in perfect peace, because He trusted his father to get them to the other side. Jesus illustrated faith in action, whereas, the disciples illustrated unbelief in action.

Let me explain that it's the time between the promise and its manifestation that the conflict between flesh and Spirit rages. If we are going to silence the inner battle and make the right choice, we must remember who God is. We must consider that He never lies. He always performs his promises in his time, and this storm or trial is part of the overcoming that we must do to inherit all things (Revelation 21:7).

It's obvious the disciples at that time had no idea of the flesh and Spirit conflict. They didn't realize the inner battle of choice was raging. Their lack of knowledge caused them to yield to the flesh, become fearful, and forget the promise that they were all to go to the other side.

God's soldiers, today, have the Bible and the examples of those who have endured storms. Those who made it looked beyond the storm, the trial, the wait, the obstacle, and saw the promise of God. Such examples of enduring the storm and overcoming are seen in Joseph, Joshua, Caleb, etc.

During seedtime (when the promise is given) to the harvest (the manifestation of the promise) is when the flesh and Spirit conflict can become a raging storm. The inner battle of choice will have us in turmoil as the conflict becomes unnerving.

We begin to question if we really heard from God. We begin to question if God's word is true. We begin to look at the storm (as the disciples did), and forget about what God has done in the past. In other words, we can become filled with unbelief as we look at the walled cities and the giants we must face in the promise land.

If the enemy can cause us to doubt God, we make the wrong choice. As Israel, we will decide not to trust God. We all know what they missed by believing the evil report and not believing God would give them the victory.

It's during the conflict of flesh and Spirit that we must remember God's word and choose to hang on no matter what the enemy comes at us with. Only as we remember God's word, his promises, what He's done in the past, that He's all-powerful, etc., will we, by faith, deny our flesh, yield to the Spirit, and win the inner battle of choice between faith and unbelief!

Chapter 5

Man's First Effects of Choice

And God said, Let us make man in our image, after our
likeness: and let them have dominion over the fish of the sea,
and over the fowl of the air, and over the cattle, and over all
the earth, and over every creeping thing that creepeth upon
the earth. So God created man in his own image, in the image
of God created he him; male and female created he them.

GENESIS 1:26–27

And the Lord God commanded the man, saying, Of every
tree of the garden thou mayest freely eat: But of the tree of
the knowledge of good and evil, thou shalt not eat of it: for
in the day that thou eatest thereof thou shalt surely die.

GENESIS 2:16–17

BEFORE WE GET INTO the effects of choice, let's understand that man
was created in the image and likeness of God. Although the image
and likeness means that we are a resemblance, model, or similitude

of God, for this chapter, we'll concentrate on our attributes—our inner nature—our ability to make choices.

When God created us in his image and likeness, the inherent qualities of God, his characteristics, his nature or quality were placed in mankind. Both men (male) and women (female) were created to have the quality of God existing in them.

Being created in the image of God, we were endowed with intellect and will. Our *intellect* is the faculty of the mind to reason, think, and know. It's the understanding or comprehending whatever is communicated whether seen, heard, read, etc. Our *will* is the faculty of the mind by which we CHOOSE what to do.

God made us a free moral agent capable of making a choice. We decide what we believe and what we choose. As a free moral agent, it's our free-will that chooses what action we take and what we believe. We choose to do good or evil, to be virtuous or vicious, to love or hate, to be kind or unkind, to obey God or disobey him, to listen to faith or unbelief, etc.

Now since man was created for God's glory, we could best glorify God by freely choosing his will over ours, choosing faith over unbelief, choosing to yield to the Spirit and not the flesh.

That's why it was essential for Adam and Eve to be given the opportunity to make such a choice. God desires that his crowned creation choose to obey, choose to worship, and choose his will because we love him more than self.

God didn't create mankind to be merely his creation. He created us to be his family. Because of his perfect love, He gave us a free-will to choose to love, to worship, to obey him, etc. There are no puppets, pawns, etc. in the kingdom of God. All of his children are free-will agents who have chosen Christ Jesus as Savior out of love for God.

Once we comprehend the love of God for us, it does something in our heart that causes us to love him more than our very life. If the love of God is not understood, please read chapter 3 of my book, *Storms Are Faith's Workout* for illumination.

> And the Lord God commanded the man, saying, Of every tree of the garden thou mayest freely eat, But of the

tree of the knowledge of good and evil, thou shalt not
eat of it: for in the day that thou eatest thereof thou shalt
surely die (Genesis 2:16–17).

So, the Garden of Eden was not only a paradise, but a place of proba-
tion. They were tested to see if they would choose God or self (flesh).

Pay attention. Of all the trees in the garden, only one was
forbidden. But one was all Satan needed. He came in the form of
a serpent, beguiling, cunning, and deceiving. Let's not forget that
Satan had already beguiled one third of the angels to fall with him
(Revelation 12:4).

> Now the serpent was more subtle than any beast of the
> field which the Lord God had made. And he said unto the
> woman, Yea, hath God said, Ye shall not eat of every tree
> of the garden? And the woman said unto the serpent, We
> may eat of the fruit of the trees of the garden: But of the
> fruit of the tree which is in the midst of the garden, God
> hath said, Ye shall not eat of it, neither shall ye touch it,
> lest ye die. And the serpent said unto the woman, Ye shall
> not surely die: For God doth know that in the day ye eat
> thereof, then your eyes shall be opened, and ye shall be as
> gods, knowing good and evil. And when the woman saw
> that the tree was good for food, and that it was pleasant
> to the eyes, and a tree to be desired to make one wise, she
> took of the fruit thereof, and did eat, and gave also unto
> her husband with her: and he did eat (Genesis 3:1–6).

In the Garden, Adam and Eve lived in a state of innocence and un-
broken communion with God. There was no sin in the man or his
wife, but when Satan tempted this first couple, they disobeyed God.
Their sin brought the curse of sin and death upon mankind from
that time forward.

Let's start to comprehend what happened in the Garden. How
did the sin come about? As we look at Genesis 3:1–6, we see that
Satan encouraged doubt about what God said in Eve's mind. The
devil's lie caused her to doubt God's motives and guidelines.

One of the primary sins is that of unbelief in God's word.
It's questioning or doubting if He really means what He says. Let's
think about it, how many today are teaching that a God of love will

never send anyone to Hell? How many are teaching that saying the sinner's prayer gives license to sin because all sins were forgiven (past, present, and future) on Calvary?

I won't go into that in this book, because I addressed that issue in my books, *Spiritual Shipwreck on the Horizon* and *Signs of the Time*. For this book, we'll concentrate on the conflict of our flesh against Spirit and our inner battle to make the right choice.

As we look at Adam and Eve, we see they made the wrong choice to which we are the recipients of. Their temptation is what we all encounter. We cannot confront any temptation uncommon to all of mankind (1 Corinthians 10:13).

Remember that temptation is not sin. This is seen in the temptation of Christ (Matthew 1:11). It's the giving into the temptation that's sin. Whenever we know to do good and choose not to, it's sin (James 4:17).

> For all that is in the world, the lust of the flesh, and the lust of the eyes, and the pride of life, is not of the Father, but is of the world (1 John 2:16).

According to James 1:14, man is tempted when he is drawn away of his own *lust* and enticed. This is the key to how we make the wrong choice. When the conflict of flesh and Spirit causes the inner battle of choice to rage, the lust of our flesh wants to be satisfied.

Eve saw the fruit was good for food (the lust of the flesh), was pleasant to the eyes (the lust of the eyes), and desired to make one wise (pride of life). She was overcome by her own lust and enticed. When her lust conceived, it brought forth sin, and sin when it was finished, brought forth death (James 1:15).

After they disobeyed or sinned against God, their circumstances changed immediately. Satan's lie was instantly evident. They had been like God before they sinned because they were created in his image. Now, they were no longer like their Creator: God is incapable of sin.

What I want to reveal at this time is something the Lord has shown me. We understand that Adam was with Eve when she partook of the fruit (and gave also to her husband with her).

Many have taught that Adam should not have eaten, because it wasn't until he ate that the eyes of them both were opened. Although this is true, Scripture tells that Eve was deceived, but Adam was not (1 Timothy 2:14).

What caused Adam to *willfully* disobey God? Let's consider that he was convinced if they ate the forbidden fruit death would occur. So, Adam watches Eve eat, and she's fine. She didn't die. Did he think God lied to him? Did he think God was holding back something good from him? Was he enticed or drawn away by his own lust to be like God? Satan said that eating the fruit would make one like God.

We need to think about what goes through our mind during the conflict between flesh and Spirit and the inner battle of choice raging in us. Are we listening to our flesh and the lies of the devil, or are we listening to the Spirit? Are we believing God's word or believing the storm of lies? Is faith or unbelief rising up in us?

The other important factor is whether we put ourselves in the situation to be tempted. Adam was there when Eve was tempted, and he stood silently while the devil deceived her. His lust enticed him to disobey God. Have we allowed ourselves to be in a place where we can be tempted? In other words, if we had a problem with alcohol, are we at a drunken party? If we had a problem with drugs, are we around drug addicts? If we had a problem with homosexuality, are we around homosexuals? Simply put, are we, with full knowledge, allowing ourselves be put in the position to be tempted when God did not lead us there?

We can see that man's first test of choice was not the choosing of faith, but of unbelief. It was not Spirit, but flesh. It was not obedience to God, but disobedience. It was not believing truth, but lies. It was not love for God, but love of self.

Listen to me, if we don't love God more than our life, or believe that He loves us, or that the word of God is trustworthy, we will waver when tested. That's what happened to Adam and Eve. They allowed unbelief in what God said to sway them to be deceived by the devil's lie and surrender to the lust of their flesh.

Let's really comprehend the effects of Adam and Eve's choice. With their fall, Adam and Eve became subject to sin, sickness, disease, and death. They were thrown out of paradise. They were no longer in fellowship with God.

To me, the saddest effect of sin is to be out of fellowship with God. Whenever the conflict between flesh and Spirit has the inner battle of choice raging, our choice has two effects. It's either to remain in fellowship with God or to be out of fellowship with him.

I'm not saying that we will always make the right choice when the inner battle of choice is raging. There are variables at the time of the temptation. Are we where we shouldn't be? Have we purposely chosen to do what we know is against God's word? Do we love someone or something more than God? Do we study the Scriptures to know what is right or wrong according to God? Do we pray without ceasing? Are we easily tempted by the lust of our flesh, the lust of our eyes, and the pride of life? Have we practiced self-denial or self-indulgence? What I'm saying is that it's our choice to yield to the flesh or to the Spirit. It's our choice to sin against God or not to sin against God. It's our choice to believe God or the devil.

We, as Adam and Eve, are free-will agents who decide the effects, consequences, outcome, results of our choices. Is the pleasure of sin for a season worth being out of fellowship with God? If we die in that so-called pleasure unrepented, we will be out of fellowship with God for eternity.

The effects of choice are either positive or negative. Our wrong choices have negative effects that can have eternal consequences. It means we yield to the flesh, choose unbelief, and renounce fellowship with God. Positive means we keep the faith, yield to the Spirit, and remain in fellowship with God. As we realize the consequences of wrong choices, it should inspire us to deny our flesh what it wants and choose to obey God!

Chapter 6

There's No Peace In the Flesh

Peace I leave with you, my peace I give unto you, not
as the world giveth, giveth I unto you. Let not your
heart be troubled, neither let it be afraid.

JOHN 14:27

These things have I spoken unto you, that in me ye might
have peace. In the world ye shall have tribulation: but
be of good cheer; I have overcome the world.

JOHN 16:33

Be careful for nothing, but in everything by prayer and supplication
with thanksgiving, let your requests be made known unto
God. And the peace of God which passeth all understanding,
shall keep your hearts and minds through Christ Jesus.

PHILIPPIANS 4:6–7

THIS IS A DAY of a lack of self-control. Although excesses have always existed, not to far back in time, men were more religious, and morals were important.

With moral standards being high in general, and the majority holding to a belief in God, much immoderations were kept in restraint. Self-control seemed to be the normal and self-indulgence the abnormal.

Let me tell you, if I didn't know the man of sin has not been revealed, I would believe the restraining power of God in withholding had been taken out of the way as stated in 2 Thessalonians 2:6–12.

Sin, corruption, evil, wickedness are rampant as never before. Yet, 2 Thessalonians 2 makes clear it will get worse when the restraining power is taken out of the way.

Now, the restraining power is not removed and yet morality and religion seem to be removed at times. What is the answer for the extreme lack of self-control or denying of self?

> Now the Spirit speaketh expressly, that in the latter times some shall depart from the faith, giving heed to seducing spirits, and doctrines of devils: Speaking lies in hypocrisy; having their conscience seared with a hot iron (1 Timothy 4:1–2).

We see why sin is much more out of control. Many have left the true faith in God based on his Son's sacrificial death and are basing their faith on whatever sounds good to their flesh. In other words, we have more itching ear preachers and teachers because that's what people are heaping to themselves. Why is that so?

> This know also, that in the last days perilous times shall come. For men shall be lovers of their own selves, covetous, boasters, proud, blasphemers, disobedient to parents, unthankful, unholy, without natural affection, trucebreakers, false accusers, incontinent, fierce, despisers of those that are good, traitors, heady, highminded, lovers of pleasures more than lovers of God (2 Timothy 3:1–4).

> Yea, and all that will live godly in Christ Jesus shall suffer persecution. But evil men and seducers shall

wax worse and worse, deceiving and being deceived
(2 Timothy 3:12–13).

Let's look at this truth. Abortion (murder of babies) is considered
normal because it will be an inconvenience to have a child. Homosexuality is promoted as a legitimate lifestyle and legalized by
our Supreme Court. Transgender is being taught to elementary
children. Yet, the Bible makes clear that it's all sin. God knows us
before we're formed in the belly (Jeremiah 1:5), and thou shalt not
kill (Exodus 20:13). Homosexuality is an abomination to God (Le-
viticus 18:22). God created ONLY male and female (Genesis 5:2),
He made no mistake and created a male inside a female or a female
inside a male. A male is not born with a uterus or ovaries to produce eggs, therefore, he is not a female inside a male body. A female
is not born without a uterus or ovaries to produce eggs, therefore,
she is not a male inside a female body.

The dark web is promoting the assassination of our president. Many liberals are encouraging the same thing. How wicked,
evil, and debauched have many become to promote the murder of
a president? Well, I guess, if they think nothing of murdering an
innocent baby, murdering someone they don't agree with is how
debased they have become.

Listen to me, it all stems because of the lust of the flesh and indulging its every whim. There's no denying self, but self-indulgence
of murder, rape, child rape, or whatever debauched thought comes
into the mind.

What does debauched mean? It's depraved, degenerate, corrupt, immoral, self-indulgent, etc. It's a leading away from morals
to corruption. In other words, it's the basis for being given over to a
reprobate mind (Romans 1:24–28).

> Men's hearts failing them for fear, and for looking after
> those things which are coming on the earth (Luke 21:26).

This world is not a nice place to be, but we are here. If we don't want
to go down with its corruption and be overcome by it all, God's soldiers had better look up to the hills from whence cometh our help.
Our help cometh from the Lord, which made heaven and earth. He

will not suffer thy foot to be moved, he that keepeth thee will not slumber (Psalm 121:1–3).

Christ is our peace. This is the foundation upon which we must begin to comprehend how to overcome all that is coming upon this earth.

Grasping God's peace takes time, because it involves the denying of self. We must learn to deny our flesh its lust of fear, worry, anxiety, etc. Only as we yield to the Spirit will there be no fear, no worry, no anxiety, etc. It's the peace of God which passeth all understanding that will keep our hearts and minds to overcome this world with its havoc, evil, wickedness, debauchery, etc.

How many reading this chapter could at this time give me an explanation or a description of God's peace? Many would say, "It passes all understanding." Although, that's a true biblical answer, but that wouldn't help us to understand what God's peace is.

A Biblical or theological dissertation sounds really great, but unless the concept, the precept, the principle is understood, we'll never really know the peace of God.

Behind the peace of God is a secret, the hidden truth, or the key so-to-speak. What is the secret to God's Peace? It's summed up in one word *TRUST*, and trust means faith. They are synonymous.

This trust is not some superficial trust, but one that puts itself totally, completely, wholly in God's hands. To explain, I'll give my all-time example. If you read *Storms Are Faith's Workout*, you'll remember this story.

> A tight rope is placed across Niagara Falls. A man asks the crowd of spectators, "Do you believe that I can walk across and back again on the tightrope?" The crowd all reply in the affirmative. He walks across and back again, and the people are cheering. Next, he asks, "Do you believe that I can push a wheelbarrow across and back again?" They are excited by this time, and all shout their affirmation. He then proceeds to push it across and back. The crowd is beside themselves with enthusiasm. They are cheering, clapping, and jumping up and down. Once he quiets the crowd, he asks, "Do you believe I can push a person in this wheelbarrow across and back again?" The

crowd is out of control by this time with shouting and cheering. He then shouts, "Who will be my first volunteer?" A hush falls over the crowd. Complete silence. He asked again. Not a one volunteered. Their flesh coiled at the thought.

Listen to me. That's exactly what trusting God can feel like on the flesh. It's not just claiming to believe. It's getting in the wheelbarrow with knees knocking. That means, butterflies galore, heart pumping, etc. We know once we step into that wheelbarrow, we must sit still. If we step out, it's down the falls we go.

After a while, in spite of our flesh, we lay back and rest in the wheelbarrow and keep our eyes focused up to Heaven and don't dare look down at the destructive falls. It's remembering to keep our eyes on Jesus and off the storm. It's being like Jesus asleep in the boat while the storm is raging. It's knowing that God is in control, and He will get us through the storm. In other words, we lay back and let the water take us into land.

Let me explain something to help us understand God's peace. I was a nervous wreck for many years. My nerves were shot as a child. The doctor put me on tranquillizers at the age of fourteen. It probably would have been sooner, but that's when I was finally taken to a doctor. If you've read my book, *Storms Are Faith's Workout*, I tell some of my childhood that will help you to understand why I was in such a state.

Anyway, I worried about everything. I was ridiculous. I worried what everyone thought of me. I worried about things of the past. I worried about what could or might happen today, tomorrow, next year, etc. I was sick with worry, fear, anxiety. After I became saved, I was a little better, but it took time to learn that God has my life in his hands.

As time went on, my knowledge grew in the word. I asked the Lord to help me understand the peace that passeth all understanding. I wanted to do a message on it as so many were in such turmoil in their lives. So, I asked God to explain what it was. I needed to know what his peace was. I asked, "Lord, what is the peace of God? What is your Peace? Lord, I know Jesus is our peace and it passeth all understanding. I know the world can't give it to me either. But what is it? How do I relate it to others?"

He spoke to my heart and said, "It's what you've been experiencing as a result of learning to trust me."

I was dumbfounded, and asked what He meant. He told me to think and back-up to a year or so earlier. He showed me all the worries I had about being able to minister. I questioned if I could even preach and teach his word. I worried about my son, my daughters, my family, our bills, the people I pastored or counselled, my studies, etc. In short, everything was an anxiousness for me. Overwhelming worry and nervousness.

He asked me how I stopped all that nervous anxiety. I explained that his word says that He's not a man that He can lie. Whatever He promises, He is able to keep or perform. He had taught me to put all things to the side and concentrate wholeheartedly on seeking the Kingdom of God and His righteousness. He taught me that worry only makes things worse. He taught me that He loves me and has my life in his hands. There are no safer hands to be in than his. In short, He had taught me to trust that He has all things in control.

It became more important to me to bear fruit, to trust him, and to know his word. Then I realized that I had been living or experiencing the peace of God, because I trusted him. I focused on him and not the storms or problems. I learned to stand on his promises instead of looking at the storm.

Before I learned to trust him, I would be in the flesh and cry, beg, plead day in and day out to fulfill his call, my son's salvation, the salvation of my family members, the bills getting paid, etc.

What happened to change my focus was something He'd asked me. He asked me if I could change my stature or add hair to my head. Of course, I couldn't do such a thing. All I knew is that prayer changes things, so I kept praying.

He answered, "I change things when the prayer of faith is given. When you pray in my will." I told him that it was his will for me to fulfill my call, my son's salvation, that we owe no man anything, finish my degrees, etc.

He replied that my worry and anxiety was sin. It's unbelief. He doesn't move in unbelief, because it revealed that I didn't trust him.

Instead of yielding to the Spirit, I was yielding to the flesh and living in fear and not faith. There can be no peace in fear.

I had to learn that *trust* and *faith* go hand in hand. We can't say we believe or have faith in God while worrying or being fearful, etc. If we're to experience God's peace, we have to trust him, while we sit in the wheelbarrow, while the ship is filling with water, while the storms of life are raging, while we don't understand any of it, etc.

What we have to comprehend, we can't calm the storm around us if the storm is raging in us. Jesus was able to get up and say, "Peace, be still" to the storm because He had the peace of God inside him. The disciples were in the flesh, and couldn't calm the storm around them because of the storm of fear and unbelief engulfing them.

If we're going to win the inner battle of choice for the Lord, we must remember that trust is something we do even if it didn't turn out like we prayed. When we see a loved one in the hands of the devil. When it looks like everything is going under. When we don't think we can go on. When the conflict of flesh and Spirit has the inner battle of choice raging, is the time we choose to deny our flesh, get into that wheelbarrow, and lie back. We know there's no peace in the flesh!

Chapter 7

Giant Slayers

Trust in the Lord with all thine heart; and lean
not unto thine own understanding.

P ROVERBS 3:5

And they went and came to Moses, and to Aaron, and to all the
congregation of the children of Israel, unto the wilderness of Paran,
to Kadesh; and brought back word unto them, and unto all the
congregation, and shewed them the fruit of the land. And they told him,
and said, We came unto the land whither thou sentest us, and surely
it floweth with milk and honey; and this is the fruit of it. Nevertheless
the people be strong that dwell in the land, and the cities are walled,
and very great: and moreover we saw the children of Anak there. The
Amalekites dwell in the land of the south: and the Hittites, and the
Jebusites, and Amorites, dwell in the mountains: and the Canaanites
dwell by the sea, and by the coast of Jordan. And Caleb stilled the
people before Moses, and said, Let us go up at once, and possess it; for
we are well able to overcome it. But the men that went up with him
said, We be not able to go up against the people; for they are stronger
than we. And they brought up an evil report of the land which they had

searched unto the children of Israel, saying, The land, through which we
have gone to search it, is a land that eateth up the inhabitants thereof;
and all the people that we saw in it are men of a great stature. And there
we saw giants, the sons of Anak, which come of the giants: and we
were in our own sight as grasshoppers, and so we were in their sight.

NUMBERS 13:26–33

And all the congregation lifted up their voice, and cried, and the
people wept that night. And all the children of Israel murmured
against Moses and against Aaron: and the whole congregation said
unto them, Would God that we had died in the land of Egypt! Or
would God we had died in this wilderness! And Joshua the son of Nun,
and Caleb the son of Jephunneh, which were of them that searched
the land, rent their clothes: And they spake unto all the company of
the children of Israel, saying, The land, which we passed through to
search it, is an exceeding good land. If the Lord delight in us, then
he will bring us into this land, and give it us; a land which floweth
with milk and honey. Only rebel not ye against the Lord, neither
fear ye the people of the land; for they are bread for us: their defence
is departed from them, and the Lord is with us: fear them not.

NUMBERS 14:1–2, 2:6–9

THIS CHAPTER WILL HELP us understand how fear is the main cause
of yielding to the flesh and not the Spirit. Instead of slaying the giants of unbelief, many are overcome by fear at their enormous size.
Whenever we give into the flesh, the inner battle of choice chooses to
fear the giant instead of remembering our God supersedes all giants.

Although we should all know this story, I will mention some
points to reveal how we can allow ourselves to listen to an evil report that will bring forth fear and unbelief.

These are the people that God miraculously delivered from
Egyptian bondage. The same people who had experienced the
phenomenal crossing of the Red Sea on dry land. This is the same

people the Lord had made the incredible promise at the Red Sea that He'd fight for them. Now, let's look at the Scripture promise.

> And Moses said unto the people, Fear ye not, stand still, and see the salvation of the Lord, which he will shew to you today: for the Egyptians whom ye have seen today, ye shall see them again no more forever. The Lord shall fight for you, and ye shall hold your peace (Exodus 14:13–14).

God promised to fight for them. He showed them his ability by parting the Red Sea and drowning all the Egyptians. All they had to do was walk on the dry land across to the other side. These same people declared in Exodus 15 through song: "The Lord is my strength and song, and he is become my salvation. He is my God!"

The main point is after all that, they missed out on God's promises because of choosing to murmur, complain, etc. When the flesh and Spirit conflict confronted them, they yielded to the flesh. They gave up the battle and chose fear and unbelief. Each trial they faced, the giants of unbelief were always mightier than God.

The sad truth is that they forgot how God delivered them from every obstacle they faced. If they were hungry, He supplied manna. If they were thirsty, He supplied water. Plus, their clothes and shoes never waxed old for the forty years of wandering (Deuteronomy 29:5).

Okay, let's go on. Before we were born again, we were in bondage and Satan was our master. And he's a terrible taskmaster. Satan always takes, he never gives. His goal or desire is to destroy God's ultimate creation which is us. Thus, he's always stealing, killing, and destroying (John 10:10).

We are the only creation created in God's image. We are special to God and the devil hates us for it. Let me explain what Satan wants.

1. Satan doesn't want us worshiping God—he wants us worshiping him.

2. Satan doesn't want us believing God's promises—he wants us believing his lies.

3. Satan doesn't want us believing God's bigger than giants—he wants us fearing his giants.

4. Satan doesn't want us enjoying God's freedom—he wants us kept in bondage.

5. Satan doesn't want us living in God's blessings—he wants us living in want and lack.

The greatest tool the devil uses to keep us from God's promises is to keep us in some kind of bondage, whether sin in our life, fear, doubt, unbelief, unforgiveness, jealousy, envy, covetousness, lying, stealing, sexual sin, etc. As long as he can convince us the giant is too big for us, we don't taste the abundant life of living in the land flowing with milk and honey. God wants us to comprehend that He desires us to live our life in the fulness of his promises. God wants us calm and not living in fear. God wants us forgiving and not living in unforgiveness. God wants us truthful and not living in lies. God wants us blessed and not living in wretchedness. God wants us to have faith and not living in unbelief. That's why Satan works over-time to keep us focused on the giant that prevents us from enjoying the fulness of God's promises.

In our Scripture texts, we see there were ten spies with an evil (flesh) report, and two with a faith (Spirit) report. Let me interject a little biblical numerology. The number ten means trial or testing, whereas, the number two means a witness or testimony.

It was a test to see whose report the people would believe when the flesh and Spirit conflict was raging. If we look at it logically, we see there's more evidence in favor of the lie. That means, ten to two. But faith yields to the Spirit and believes God.

> Now, faith is the substance of things hoped for, the evidence of things not seen (Hebrews 11:1).

Let's examine the contradictory claim of the evil report. They claim the land surely flows with milk and honey. We're told in Numbers 13:23 the cluster of grapes was so huge that two men had to carry it between them on a staff. Plus they brought back pomegranates and figs. The substance of the fruit should have spoken volumes to this people of the blessings God wanted them to enjoy. Furthermore, how did they spy out the land and get out without being seen?

Instead of remembering all God had done or even thinking how he protected them to spy out the land for forty days, they mention walled cities. Now, mind you, this is the same people who recently crossed the Red Sea on dry land with the waters heaped like mountains on either side.

Then they complain the land is full of giants, and we're merely grasshoppers next to them. Remember when they crossed the Red Sea, God promised to fight for them. They had the proof of the Egyptians who drowned when trying to pursue them.

Now, the faith report of Joshua and Caleb reaffirmed it was a good land. They believed God would give them the land and told the people not to rebel against the Lord and not to fear the people.

Why did Joshua and Caleb tell them not to fear? They claimed their defense was departed from the Canaanites because the Lord was with Israel. These two faithful spies knew and believed God's promise to fight for them. They knew if God before them, who could be against them. (Romans 8:31). There was no giant that God couldn't conquer or slay.

Okay, what is the intention of this chapter? It's quite simple. Many of God's soldiers are not denying self when the battle rages within between flesh and Spirit. Because of compromise and a lack of fortitude, we end up yielding to the flesh and are left looking at the giant of despair. When we do that we end up like Christian and Hopeful as prisoners in Doubting Castle by Giant Despair in John Bunyan's "The Pilgrim's Progress."

When this occurs, we are in a quagmire of storms, facing mountainous obstacles, and barraged by Satan's strategies to destroy our faith in God. This is why many of God's soldiers are imprisoned in Doubting Castle overwhelmed by Giant Despair and not living in the promises of God.

Let's make something clear. Our giant trials, storms, obstacles, strategies of the enemy are common in our faith journey. What I'm trying to get us to comprehend is the consequences of yielding to the flesh and not the Spirit when faced with which road to take. Do we go the way of the flesh (the road to Doubting Castle and imprisonment by Giant Despair), or do we go the way of the Spirit (the road to overcoming all giants through faith in God)?

What we must grasp is that we always face storms, obstacles, and strategies. To think otherwise is to be deceived. We are the overcomers through him that loves us. If we allow unbelief to overtake us, we will never experience God's promises.

There are *thousands of promises* in the Bible that reveal God's eternal purposes to which He is unchangeably committed to fulfill. God's soldiers can totally depend upon him to do as He promises. However, these promises are conditional upon obedience on our part. We can't expect God to keep a promise when we disobey and rebel against his word.

Let me explain. Isaiah 1:19 says, "If ye be willing and obedient, ye shall eat the good of the land." That's quite clear that we only eat of the good of the land IF we're willing and obedient.

Now, back to the Israelites to keep building our understanding of what happens when we yield to our flesh and not the Spirit. After they believed the evil report, we're aware they walked through the wilderness for forty years until all the disbelievers over twenty were dead. Hebrews 3:19 informs us they didn't enter the promise land because of unbelief.

What is unbelief? According to Romans 14:23, whatsoever is not of faith is sin. Thus, unbelief is sin. Why did they have unbelief? Why did they fear? Why did they doubt God?

1. Unbelief resulted from believing the evil report.

2. They feared the giants more than they trusted God.

3. Doubt resulted because they refused to hear the faith report which should have quickened them to what God had already done.

4. They forgot the plagues of Egypt and their protection from them, they forgot their Egyptian bondage and deliverance, they forgot the Red Sea deliverance.

It all boils down to the fact that they didn't trust God, which brings us to the first part of our Scripture text in *Proverbs 3:5* informing us to trust in the Lord with all our heart. This implies to believe God's promise with our whole heart, and to look for its fulfillment without doubt, without fear, and without distrust.

Trust means to be confident in, to be secure, to be without fear. To be firm and certain. Let's put it this way. God wants us to believe with our whole heart in his promise, whatever it is. We need to be firm and certain in him and in his word. We are to have no doubt, no fear, no distrust. To be firm and certain means firm doesn't waiver, and certain doesn't doubt. If we are not firm and certain, we will lose the inner battle of choice to our flesh. In doing so, we'll focus on the giant and not receive whatever promise God has given us.

Listen to me. It's during the flesh and Spirit conflict that we must remember God's word. His word claims that we can do all things through Christ which strengtheneth us (Philippians 4:13), with God nothing shall be impossible (Luke 1:37), my God shall supply all your need according to his riches in glory by Christ Jesus (Philippians 4:19).

Warfare is hard. It's an arduous, a laborious, and a strenuous endeavor. To win the battle over all the Canaanites (self and worldly persecution) is difficult to accomplish. We will never win over these enemies in the world, unless we have first won the battle over self. Once self is put under subjection to the will of God, the spiritual warfare against the Canaanites becomes less of a struggle. If self has been crucified with Christ, the inner battle of choice is quickly won.

If we look at the so-called giants as Israel did, we will yield to fear and despair. We will find ourselves imprisoned by Giant Despair in Doubting Castle. Whenever we give place to our flesh, it will rule and not the Spirit.

God took them through much, as He has done for us. Fear tends to paralyze. When this happens, we give place to unbelief in the magnitude or greatness of God. As God promised to fight for the Israelites, He has promised to always be with us. Why do we tend to look at the size of the giants, the storms, the obstacles, the strategies of Satan and not the enormity of our God?

> (As it is written, I have made thee a father of many nations), before him whom he believed, even God, who quickeneth the dead, and calleth those things which be not as though they were. Who against hope believed in hope, that he might become the father of many

> nations. . .And being not weak in faith, he considered
> not his own body now dead. . .neither yet the deadness
> of Sarah's womb: He staggered not at the promise of God
> through unbelief, but was strong in faith, giving glory to
> God; and being fully persuaded that what he had prom-
> ised, he was able also to perform (Romans 4:17–21).

Let's look at Abraham's giants. He was a hundred years old, and ninety year old Sarah's womb was dead. There would be no child-bearing. But Abraham when all hope, as a human possibility failed, placed his hope (trust) in God. He trusted God to call those things which be not as though they were. Abraham's faith knew that God had the ability to create out of nothing (ex nihilo). He knew where there's death, God creates life. Where there's nothing, God creates something.

This is where the rest of *Proverbs 3:5* comes in telling us not to lean unto our own understanding. The Hebrew for *lean not unto* means NOT TO SUPPORT ONE'S SELF. In other words, we are NOT to lean on self, NOT to rely on self, NOT to rest on self, and NOT to have confidence in self.

> There is a way which seemeth right unto a man, but the
> end thereof are the ways of death (Proverbs 14:12).

If Abraham had leaned on—supported himself on his fleshly understanding—Isaac would never have been born. Isaac is the result of faith in God's ability. Simply put, Isaac is the miracle of faith in God.

God's soldiers must comprehend God could not have kept his promise without Abraham's faith in him to do what He promised. We know this is also true of Sarah. Hebrews 11:11 says that through faith Sarah herself received strength to conceive seed. Whereas, Hebrews 3:19 claims the Israelites didn't enter the promise land, the fulness of God's promises, because of the sin of unbelief.

The Greek word translated for unbelief is *APISTIA* which means faithlessness, disbelief, or unfaithfulness. In simple terms, they didn't enter in because they didn't believe God. The giants of fear, doubt, and unbelief became bigger in their eyes than God's promises.

Now, Numbers 13:33 says "in our own sight, we were as grass-hoppers next to the giants." What does "own sight" imply? It means "our own understanding." They leaned upon their own understanding or fleshly logic. They didn't lean on God, they leaned on self. Whereas, Abraham and Sarah leaned on faith in God.

We need to ask ourselves, "What giant is keeping us from believing God? What giant is keeping us leaning upon our own understanding and not faith?" We must comprehend that whatever is contrary to faith in God is sin (unbelief). Unbelief will stop the promises of God from being part of our life. We cannot enter into God's promises without faith.

God's love doesn't alter for us, but our unbelief stops the flow of promises. We cannot please God without faith, believing He is, and that He will bless (Hebrews 11:6).

Let me explain this. It's a little easier for us who are parents to understand this principle. We love our children. But when they disobey, we can't reward for disobedience. Can we? Of course not. Not if we desire them to grow up as law abiding citizens. Not if we desire them to have all that God has for them. It's our responsibility to train them up in the way they should go.

We don't hold back rewards, because we don't love them. To be honest, I believe there were times it was harder on me to keep back the reward than it was on my children (they are now, fifty-two, fifty-one, and forty-nine). It's called "tough love," and it can be difficult.

Can you imagine how difficult it must be for God, whose love is perfect? How it must grieve him that He must hold back blessings because of our sin, fear, doubt, and unbelief. That's why this chapter is calling for giant slayers. The Spirit of Joshua and Caleb to rise up in the church and conquer the giant that stands in the way of receiving God's promises.

What giant is it? Is it known sin? Is it love for the things of this world? Is it fear? Is it an addiction? Is it worry? Is it a constant murmuring and complaining? Is it discontentment serving God? Is it unbelief in his ability to keep his promise?

Whatever the giant may be, we must not allow the father of lies to convince us that the giant is too big. He's the one that threw his darts to keep us in the fear, addiction, worry, complaining, discontentment, unbelief, etc. He knows unbelief receives nothing from God.

As I've told in my book, *Storms Are Faith's Workout*, there's a storm between every promise (seedtime) and the manifestation of the promise (harvest). We have been given promises and our faith is being tried through the storm.

Will we focus on the giants? Will we believe God who cannot lie or the devil who cannot tell truth? Yes, the storm has been long and laborious, but there's not a limit on the time frame of the promise and its fulfillment. Are we wavering at the promise of God? Is the giant getting bigger and bigger? Have we become weary? Is sin, worry, fear, unbelief, etc. preventing us from receiving the promise? Are we believing the evil report that the giant is to big?

God doesn't want us living in defeat, want, worry, sickness, etc. They are all lies of the devil and contrary to the promises of God. As I said, we can't bless disobedience in our children, and God can't bless disobedience in his children.

Let me tell you, I want to live in the promises of God. He doesn't withhold any good thing from those that walk uprightly (Psalm 84:11). Many think that only Heaven is where we receive good things. While Heaven will be fantastic, the promises of God, in his word, are for this time. We won't need the promises in Heaven. There will be no more flesh and Spirit conflict. There will be no inner battle of choice. For there will be no more fallen nature to contend with.

Why are God's soldiers settling for the devil's lies instead of God's promises? It's quite simple. When the flesh and Spirit conflict begins, and the inner battle of choice is raging, we give into the flesh.

It's time to stop looking at the giants through unbelief. The Lord wants us to comprehend the Universe isn't big enough to contain him. There's NO giant too big that God cannot conquer. There's NO bondage that He cannot break. There's NO sickness or disease that He cannot heal. There's NO promise that He cannot keep. Only as we choose to deny self and yield to the Spirit will the inner battle of choice bring forth the faith needed to slay any giant!

Chapter 8

The War of Waiting

Who hath measured the waters in the hollow of his hand, and meted out heaven with the span, and comprehended the dust of the earth in a measure, and weighed the mountains in scales, and the hills in a balance? Who hath directed the spirit of the Lord, or being his counsellor hath taught him? With whom took he counsel, and who instructed him and taught him in the path of judgment, and taught him knowledge, and shewed to him the way of understanding?. . . Have ye not known? have ye not heard? hath it not been told you from the beginning? have ye not understood from the foundations of the earth? It is he that sitteth upon the circle of the earth, and the inhabitants thereof are as grasshoppers; that stretcheth out the heavens as a curtain, and spreadeth them out as a tent to dwell in. . .To whom then will ye liken me, or shall I be equal? saith the Holy One. Lift up your eyes on high, and behold who hath created these things, that bringeth out their host by number: he calleth them all by names by the greatness of his might, for that he is strong in power; not one faileth. Why sayest thou, O Jacob, and speakest, O Israel, My way is hid from the Lord, and my judgment is passed over from my God? Hast thou not known? hast thou not heard, that the everlasting God, the Lord, the Creator of the ends of the earth, fainteth not, neither is weary? there is no searching of his understanding. He giveth power to the faint; and to them that have no might he increaseth strength. Even the youths shall faint and be wary, and the young men shall utterly fall: *But they that wait upon the Lord shall renew their strength; they shall mount up with wings as eagles; they shall run, and not be weary; and they shall walk, and not faint.*

ISAIAH 40:12–14, 21–31

THIS CHAPTER SHOULD HELP us to comprehend the struggle that takes place between our flesh and Spirit during the times of waiting. Growing weary is the cause of many yielding to the flesh during the trial or storm of waiting.

Isaiah 40:31 has to be a Scripture that we quote over and over again. When we know God's soldier is going through a hard time we'll quote that verse. Even though we quote this verse, say it over and over again in our minds, and quote it to other people, do we fully comprehend the magnitude of what God is trying to convey to us?

I believe we don't. I say that because of the lives of defeated Christians I've witnessed in Christianity. There are many of God's soldiers living underneath their problems. Yet, God has ordained that we are more than conquerors or overcomers through him that loved us (Romans 8:37).

And yet, why are we not living as overcomers or conquerors? Why are we not above all our situations? Why do our troubles or our problems seem to bring us under and keep us in bondage if Jesus has set us free? (John 8:36)

Let's look at our Scripture text in Isaiah to understand. These verses were written to the captives in Babylon. God's people had been taken captive and they were in Babylon. Now, they were at the place where they had forgotten the magnitude or the awesomeness and greatness of their God, and they were turning to idols.

As we study the verses in Isaiah 40, we will see they had turned from serving God and they were watching the Babylonians. Their captives were a powerful Nation that was great and powerful. As

Israel looked upon them, they began to consider their gods. They began to think the gods of Babylon were incredibly great. Yet, they were gods made by the hands of man. These idols or gods were man-made.

Because Israel was oppressed, in captivity, in bondage, they began to believe their God was not big enough or great enough to deliver them. They had forgotten the word of God. They had forgotten the great deliverance from the Egyptian bondage. They forgot about the blood on the two side posts and on the upper door post had caused the death angel to Passover. They forgot how God delivered Noah and his family from the flood. They had forgotten all the wondrous things God had done.

Why did they forget God's promises and his past deliverances? Because they did what many of God's soldiers are doing today. They looked at the giant, the problems, the storm, etc. Whenever we look at the storm, we will sink like Peter (Matthew 14:30).

How many of us are looking at our problems, our financial problems, our marital problems, our rebellious children, our problems at work, our problems at school, our sickness and seeing them as giants? How many of us have taken our eyes off Christ and are focused on the struggles and see them as giants that we cannot conquer or overcome?

How many of us have forgotten what a great, big, wonderful God we serve? How many of us have forgotten our God is able to deliver us from all our struggles? How many of us have forgotten our God is greater and bigger than any giant we may face?

It doesn't matter how many times God warns us against worshipping other gods or worshipping idols. Because when we get into a struggle, many times we turn to people and not God. Or we turn to some sort of vice or whatever. We turn to everything or everyone, but our God who is the only one capable of delivering us out of the struggle.

Yes, there are times we need a helping hand or an ear to listen to us. But that helping hand or listening ear is not going to get into our soul, revive us, and give us the strength to conquer or overcome the struggle.

Let's continue with our Scripture text to fully understand what God wants to reveal to us. Verse 12 asks us, "Whom hath measured the waters in the hollow of his hand and meted out the heavens with the span?"

God wants his people to comprehend how great He is. God can take all the water that is in the ocean, the seas, the lakes, the rivers, the wells, etc. and put it in the hollow of his hand. Think of that. How much water can we hold in the hollow (palm) of our hand? Yet, our God can take all the water in the Universe and hold it in the hollow of his hand.

Then it says, "Who has meted out the heavens with a span?" A span is the width from the tip of the thumb to the tip of the pinky. Think of that. God meted or measured the heavens between his thumb and pinky. How much can we measure with that distance?

Now, if God can grasp everything between his thumb and pinky, what is that revealing about our God? In Isaiah 40, God wants us to realize how great He is and how wonderful He is. He wants us to understand how little we can do and how much He can do.

That's why God wants to know why his soldiers are not letting him do it. Why is He not in control of our life? Why do we try to go in our own strength? Why do we try to do things in our own power? He wants us to understand that we cannot conquer or overcome in our strength or power.

In verse 25, God asks, "To whom then will ye liken me, or shall I be equal?" In other words, He wants to know who or what can we measure him with. What or who measures up to God? He just showed that He can take all the waters in the earth and put them in the hollow of his hand. He can take the whole world and use it as a baseball. Who else can do that?

What can we measure God against? Why do God's soldiers form all these idols? Why do we make idols of people who are formed or created by God? Let's face it, they can hold no more water in the hollow of their hand than we can. Their grasp is as limited as ours. Why do we allow ourselves to look elsewhere and not to God? All things were created by the greatness of God. He is the great one. That's not pride on God's part, it's truth or fact. He can do nothing but tell truth. He is incapable of lying (Titus 1:2).

I want to interject something I saw on social media recently. This person was saying they had prayed about something and were now seeking a prophet. I was saddened and wondered what's going on with God's soldiers? We can't hear from God, so we need to seek a person for an answer. No wonder, we have so much confusion in the church. It's the Holy Spirit who guides us into all truth (John 16:13). We have God, the Holy Spirit, living in us. Why are we seeking a man/woman who can hold no more water in their hand than we can? Why are we seeking a man/woman who can't hold any more in the span of their hand than we can?

These verses in Isaiah are to help us comprehend the vastness of our God. That's why He asks us to, "Lift up your eyes on high, and behold who hath created these things, that bringeth out their host by number: He calleth them all by name, by the greatness of his might, for that He is strong in power; not one faileth."

If we begin to doubt, if we begin to wonder, and we think to look to man, we are to lift up our eyes. We are to consider all the wonderful creation and the one who created them. Who is greater than our God? Can we speak the worlds into existence? Can any man/woman we know speak the worlds into existence? God did. He said, "Let there be," and there was. Can we say let there be, and it's created? Then He says that He upholds all things by the word of his power (Hebrews 1:3).

> Through faith we understand that the worlds were framed
> by the word of God, so that things which are seen were
> not made of things which do appear (Hebrews 11:3).

What we have to recognize is that when God spoke all things into existence, He commanded to appear what did not before exist. God created all that we see out of nothing. I brought this truth forth in my book, *Satan Has No Authority Over God's Soldier*. In it, I illuminate what Godlike faith is in our life.

That's why it's important for us to grasp that faith is the substance of things hoped for, the evidence of things not seen (Hebrews 11:1). That means we don't see any evidence, we just believe. God didn't see anything, He just knew He could create it. All

He had to say was, "Let" and there was. He had the faith to believe it. That's what kind of faith He desires of us.

He wants us to say, "I don't see it, but God said or promised it. If He took nothing and made everything, surely He can bring into existence his promise to me." He's God and there's nothing impossible with him (Luke 1:37).

It's all in how we perceive God. What's our concept of God? How we comprehend him is the extent that He's enabled to move in our life. Do we perceive him as all-powerful? Do we believe that He can do all things through the degree of our faith? Do we believe He created out of nothing all that we observe in the Universe?

Is He really God in our life? Do we limit him working in our life because of unbelief? Do we underestimate his power? I believe that's the problem with many in the church. God is not truly God of our life, because we undervalue his power. I brought this truth forward in chapter 8 of my book, *Faith's Journey Confronts Obstacles*, where I revealed an episode that happened to us when remodeling a home in Connecticut.

In Isaiah 40, God is reproving Israel through the Prophet Isaiah, because they had known from the beginning. They have had the word. The Jews or Israelites were the ones who had heard from God. He'd revealed himself through Moses, the prophets, and they knew God. He'd showed himself many times through mighty signs and miracles.

Now, God is informing us that we have access to his word. We have access to the whole history of his people and the wondrous things He's done. What God did in the past, and how his people came through their storms, trials, etc., He is still the same God today that He was yesterday, and will be the same God tomorrow (Hebrews 13:8). He is able to give us the strength to slay any giant in our life, just as He did through David when facing Goliath.

God doesn't renege on his promises. It's during the war of waiting that we can become weary, start to doubt, and allow unbelief to overwhelm us. Like I revealed in my book, *Storms Are Faith's Workout*, it's the time between receiving the promise and the fulfillment that the storm WILL always appear as sure as the sun rising and setting every day.

A truly sad happening today is the ministers preaching and teaching that we don't have to have any difficulties. Our faith journey should be a tip-toe through the tulips. Well, let me tell you in my time of walking with the Lord, I've found it to be a "Rose Garden" full of thorns along with the roses. I've been pricked, jabbed, punctured time and time again. That's the reality. Denying self is NOT a tip-toe through the tulips.

Jesus revealed that fact to us. I will discuss this truth more in the next chapter. But for now, we will get pricked often. However, God is able to bind up our wounds, and enable us to smell the roses again.

Yes, there are going to be long seasons of being pricked, facing giants of despair, fierce storms, mountainous obstacles, and strategies of Satan. But as we wait upon the Lord, He shall renew our strength.

Let me explain what *renew our strength* means. In the Hebrew it implies to change for another, or to change for something better. This is the key the Lord wants us to understand during the war of waiting.

When our strength is renewed, it means our strength is changed for something better. Remember when Paul asked the Lord to take away the thorn in his flesh? The Lord told him that his grace was sufficient for his strength was made perfect in weakness.

We have to come to the place while waiting on God that we recognize our weakness. God resists the proud but gives grace to the humble (James 4:6). That means during the war of waiting or during the distress of the storm or trial that we must humble ourselves before God. We have to say to God, "Lord, I can't get through this situation in my own strength. I need you to touch my life."

During that time, God, through his grace, turns around and takes his strength and exchanges it for our weakness. In other words, our weakness is exchanged for his strength. It's exchanged for something better. The something better is God's strength, God's ability, God's grace.

That's why Paul was able to keep going even though the thorn in the flesh was uncomfortable. It's irrelevant what his thorn may have been. I believe it's not stated to help us. That way when we're facing any giant, fierce storm, mountainous obstacle, or any un-comfortable situation, we can trust God's grace to be sufficient. We can trust that He'll exchange our weakness for his strength. In other words, we can believe that He'll give us strength to go on when our strength is depleted.

How can we be strengthened if we're never tried? We're strengthened in our faith when we go through trials, because it causes us to become dependent on him. As we allow Christ to live through us, his strength becomes our strength.

It's not that He becomes weak by taking our weakness. He replaces our weakness with his strength to overcome. God never becomes tired. God never becomes sick. God never becomes weary. God is all powerful, all knowing. As we comprehend this, we give him our weakness and take his strength.

That's when we mount up as eagles. That's when we soar up there above our giants, our problems, and our difficulties. My daughter, Christina sings a song, *Master of the Wind* written by Joel Hemphill. The words say, "Sometimes I soar like an eagle through the sky. Above the peaks my soul can be found. An unexpected storm may drive me from the heights. Brings me low, but never brings me down. Chorus: I know the Master of the wind. I know the Maker of the rain. He can calm a storm, make the sun shine again. I know the Master of the wind."

We're going to find ourselves under an unexpected storm try-ing to drive us low. But, our God promises to give us his strength when we feel we can't keep going. Because we know the Master of the wind, we know He'll bring us back up to the heights above the storm to soar like an eagle.

During the war of waiting is when the conflict between flesh and Spirit can cause the inner battle of choice to become unbear-able. That's the time we could allow the giant to take us captive or in bondage to our problems and take our eyes off Christ. It's like standing at a precipice. Do we plunge into the unbelief of the flesh, or do we step back and stand on the solid ground of faith in the Spirit?

We need to comprehend that it's during the war of waiting that we can be brought low by the unexpected storm. But as we yield to the Spirit, *faith* in our God who holds all the waters of the earth in the hollow of his hand, who holds the Universe like a baseball will cause us to renew our strength or exchange our weakness for his strength. When that happens, we'll soar on high like the eagle, riding the thermal far above the war!

Chapter 9

Jesus Is Our Example

Who in the days of his flesh, when he had offered up prayers
and supplications with strong crying and tears unto him that
was able to save him from death, and was heard in that he
feared; Though he were a Son, yet learned he obedience by the
things which he suffered; And being made perfect, he became
the author of eternal salvation unto all them that obey him.

Hebrews 5:7–9

And being in an agony he prayed more earnestly: and his sweat
was as it were great drops of blood falling down to the ground.

Luke 22:44

Ye have not yet resisted unto blood, striving against sin.

Hebrews 12:4

In this chapter, we'll prayerfully comprehend why we must win
the inner battle of choice. We need to comprehend what Jesus did

for us, what He suffered, and how He chose God's will when the conflict of his flesh and Spirit was raging.

The priestly office, as marked out by God, belonged exclusively to the tribe of Levi. Yet, Jesus, although not of that tribe, was truly and properly a High Priest. He represented a different order from Aaron and executed the duties of the priesthood in a far different manner than possible for anyone to perform. Jesus didn't offer the blood of bulls and of goats, but his own body for the sins of the world.

In our Scripture texts, we perceive that never were the sufferings of any creature comparable with those of Christ. Perhaps his bodily sufferings were less than many of what some of his followers have suffered. However, the sufferings of his soul were infinitely beyond the perception of our finite minds.

The wrath of God on the sin of mankind, that He would suffer, produced that bloody sweat in the Garden of Gethsemane. The agony was so great that an angel from Heaven had to come and strengthen him (Luke 22:43–44). Jesus needed to receive physical strength to endure what was ahead at Calvary. It's imperative to comprehend that on the cross, Jesus suffered *God's wrath* so those of us who overcome will not.

Hebrews 5:7 reveals under the extreme pressure, Christ poured out his heart in prayer to his Father to save him from death.

Let me clarify something here. The fear or dread of death in Christ's flesh was beyond what mankind fears about death. We either fear the unknown or because we don't want to go.

But, Jesus was suffering for all mankind. He was taking what we should suffer for our sins upon himself. He was about to feel the wrath of God upon sin. Only God can tell how great the suffering and agony must have been for Christ in the sight of infinite justice required to make atonement for us.

I don't believe man or angels can conceive or perceive how much Jesus suffered. What's wrong with God's soldiers? Why are we so selfish? Why do we complain and consider the littlest thing as suffering? We are out of sorts if we have no sugar for our tea or coffee. Golly, what awful suffering.

> And he said to them all, if any man will come after me, let
> him deny himself, and take up his cross daily, and follow
> me (Luke 9:23).

Not too many deny self with ease. How many mistake our own selfishness as suffering? To many, it's what we want. We must be first and others must wait. We want priority over others. Let's face it, how many times have we seen people in line at the grocery store, leave their cart and walk out because of the wait? Golly, such suffering. Really, we can act worse than a two-year-old having a tantrum.

> For it is better, if the will of God be so, that ye suffer for
> well doing, than for evil doing (1 Peter 3:17).

This is another area where Christians misunderstand suffering. When we suffer because of evil doing or because we are in the wrong is not suffering but the chastening of the Lord. It's when we do what's right. It's when we put God and others before self and are persecuted, that we can claim we're suffering.

Jesus put God and all mankind, and not just the ones He got along with first. Why did He put others first? Because if He was to fulfill his earthly ministry He MUST go to Calvary. Instead of trying to avoid the suffering that was NOT rightfully or fairly his, He obediently accepted it. He understood that He must war against his flesh and win the inner battle of choice by yielding to the Spirit and choosing God's will.

What if Jesus had been like so many of God's soldiers? What if He said, "Why me? This isn't fair. Why am I being punished for what they did? I've done nothing wrong. I don't deserve this suffering." Let's face it, we can come up with all sorts of murmuring and complaints of how unjust denying self is.

As Christ's obedience became more difficult on his fleshly nature, it involved more and more self-renunciation. Even though the agony was ever increasing in severity, He still obeyed.

> And about the ninth hour Jesus cried with a loud voice,
> saying, Eli, Eli, lama sabachthani? that is to say, My God,
> my God, why hast thou forsaken me? (Matthew 27:46)

Jesus wasn't concerned about the physical pain, or dying. The agony of soul for him was the separation from his Father that He must endure for the first time in eternity. When Jesus became sin, God's wrath was poured out separating Jesus from his Father. I can't even fathom being separated from God. Yet, Jesus did it, so we won't have to be.

> But your iniquities have separated between you and your God, and your sins have hid his face from you (Isaiah 59:2).

Christ took upon himself all the sins, all the depravity, all the wickedness, etc. of mankind. He became sin which separated him from God.

Now, Hebrews 5:7 says that He was heard. This means his prayer was answered. However, it was NOT exemption from the cup. It was not exemption from the trial or the suffering. It was deliverance over his flesh to go on and put God and others first.

Jesus received victory over the dread of it. He received support in drinking the bitter cup. His fleshly weakness was exchanged for the strength of God to endure what He had to go through.

What that means is that the cup was not removed, but He was not allowed to faint or give up in drinking it. He received the necessary grace to strengthen him to withstand Calvary.

Too many of God's soldiers have the mentality that being taking out of troubles is the storm ceasing, being raptured, etc. We have to realize that God promises to give us the grace needed to exchange our weakness for his strength to get through the storm, overcome the giant, or obstacle, etc.

Hebrews 5:8–9 says that Jesus was truly the only begotten Son of the Father. Let me interject a fact here. We, as the children of God are begotten of the Father through spiritual birth. Only Jesus was begotten by God through physical birth. We are adopted sons of God. Jesus is the natural born Son of God. I inserted that because I've heard many claim that Jesus wasn't the only begotten Son of God.

Yet, even Jesus was perfected through the things He suffered. He had to go to the cross. It was necessary for him, as our High Priest, to experience everything we feel, to be tempted as we are, and to overcome without sin (Hebrews 4:15).

By being reduced to a suffering condition, He was now a partaker of the afflictions of his people. This enabled him to truly feel our infirmities and to help us when we implore his help with strong crying and tears.

Jesus didn't suffer because of selfishness or self-centeredness. He didn't suffer from sin or unrighteousness. Christ suffered because he *denied* himself and took up his cross for us.

Listen to me, if obedience to God means we must suffer the death of self, the denial of self, will we obey him? If obedience to God means that God and others are more important than "me," will we still obey him? If obedience to God means fleshly suffering, will we still obey him? If obedience to God means physical death, will we still obey him?

If we're going to overcome the conflict between flesh and Spirit and choose to do God's will during the inner battle of choice, we must deny self and take up our cross daily. It means we must get out of our self-centeredness, the "ME" syndrome and suffer the nailing of our flesh, our selfishness to the cross.

We must learn to be like Jesus and suffer self-denial. He gave no place to his flesh. The battle of his flesh and Spirit was so severe that He sweat drops of blood. How many of us have fought self to the point of sweating blood? Instead, when the battle rages, many times, we give into our will. However, only self-denial will deny our flesh, yield to the Spirit, and choose God's will during the inner battle of choice and hear, "Well done, thou good and faithful servant!"

Chapter 10

A 24–7–365 God

And the Lord went before them by day in a pillar of a cloud, to lead
them the way; and by night in a pillar of fire, to give them light;
to go by day and night. He took not away the pillar of the cloud
by day, nor the pillar of fire by night, from before the people.

Exodus 13:21–22

Lo, I am with you always, even unto the end of the world. Amen.

Matthew 28:20

For such an high priest became us, who is holy, harmless,
undefiled, separate from sinners, and made higher than
the heavens; Who needeth not daily, as those high priests,
to offer up sacrifice, first for his own sins, and then for the
people's: for this he did once, when he offered up himself.

Hebrews 7:26–27

In order to win the flesh and Spirit conflict, we need to understand that we're never alone. God doesn't allow us to face a giant by ourselves.

In football, the quarterback calls out a series of numbers before the ball is hiked. Sometimes these numbers are random. Other times they are signals, letting the other players know what play the quarterback wants run.

God's soldiers can also designate a series of numbers representing how God's presence will be played out in our lives: 24–7–365. It's not a very complex code to crack. The God revealed through our Scripture text is a 24-hours a day, a 7-days a week, a 365-days a year God. He takes NO timeouts, NO halftime breaks, and NO commercial breaks. God is present with us every moment of every day of our lives.

God can be a 24–7–365 God because Jesus was a one-time Savior. His sacrifice was once- and-for-all. Through Christ's one act of complete obedience, He became the one intercessory "priest" we need. The sacrifice Jesus made once, doesn't need to be endlessly repeated, as in the old sacrificial system.

Dietrich Bonhoeffer ran an illegal underground seminary in a remote chilly place called Finkenwalde until the Nazi's shut it down. On the altar table where the faithful worshipped every day, there was engraved a single word, *Hapax*, meaning "once." That single word focused the hearts and minds of those caught in the middle of one of history's worst nightmares on the nature of Christ's being and his sacrifice made to transform our relationship to the divine.

The message in Hebrews 7 reveals Jesus' unique identity, his perfect qualifications as our heavenly high priest, and his once-and-for-all sacrifice breathed faith and hope into the gray walls of Finkenwalde. Just as it does today for God's soldiers who find ourselves in prisons of our own making or imprisoned by forces beyond our control.

As our high priest, Jesus is constantly "on call." Jesus is 24–7–365 accessible at a "needs" notice.

> And when he heard that it was Jesus of Nazareth, he began to cry out, and say, Jesus, thou son of David, have

> mercy on me. And many charged him that he should
> hold his peace: but he cried the more a great deal, Thou
> son of David have mercy on me. And Jesus stood still,
> and commanded him to be called (Mark 10:47–49).

The healing story in Mark demonstrates how Jesus made on demand "house calls" at any time and any place. Jesus and his disciples
are starting out on the road to Jerusalem, moving toward the final
events that awaited him there. Suddenly, the cries of a blind beggar,
Bartimaeus, come ringing down the road, "Jesus, thou son of David, have mercy on me!" Despite the hushing of others, Bartimaeus
calls out again, "Jesus, thou son of David, have mercy on me!"

Hearing the blind man's cries, Jesus stops his journey. He
stands still and calls Bartimaeus to him. In response to this humble
beggar's obvious faith and persistence, Jesus publicly heals him of
his blindness.

The Bartimaeus story is noteworthy because it is the last healing miracle Jesus performs in Mark's gospel. Jesus is on the way to
Jerusalem and the cross when Bartimaeus crosses his path. In spite
of the new direction Jesus' ministry is beginning to take, he stops
and responds without hesitation to Bartimaeus's cries. Forever "on
call" Jesus could not leave a believer alone in his personal pain
and darkness. The blind beggar is healed, even though the healing intrudes upon the flow of the journey's progression towards
Jerusalem.

As our eternal accessible, always open conduit to God's mercy,
Jesus makes it possible for God's soldiers to be in an immediate,
intimate relationship with the God of the cosmos. Jesus' sacrifice
introduces us to the arms of God's mercy and takes us to the heart
of God's love.

The forgiveness Christ obtained for us brings us into our
heavenly home as full members of the divine family, where we are
protected, cherished, and taught at the knee of our divine parent.
With Jesus, we may also now address the ultimate reigning power
of the universe as "Abba" (Father).

As parents, we know that parenting is a 24–7–365 undertak-
ing. It doesn't matter if our child is 5-months, 5-years, or 50-years
old, we are ever "on call." Consider then how much more extensive

is the parental care that we may receive from God, who, as our divine parent, is in no way limited by the junctures of time and space.

As every human parent and every child knows, there are times, some experiences, where each of us must face it without the support of others. However, as long as we let Christ open the way to a personal relationship with God, there is *never* again any experience in life or death that we must face alone.

No matter how great our fear, how intense our pain, how prolonged the wait, how furious the storm, how mountainous the obstacle, how gigantic the giant, the promise of the gospel is that God is there for us. God is there alongside us 24–7–365. As God's soldiers, we never face anything alone.

Let's continue to build this chapter to explain why it's important to know that we are never alone. We are never left abandoned to fight the giants that come against us. God is with us 24–7–365.

> Thy word is a lamp unto my feet, and a light unto my path (Psalm 119:105).

Exodus 13 reveals that God gave his people light by night and day. We easily understand that light is needed at night in the physical. Although we may have natural light during the day, we can find ourselves walking in the darkness of evil. No natural light will lighten up our way. If we are to avoid the danger of being overwhelmed by the darkness, being vanquished by the giants, being destroyed during the storms, being defeated by the size of the obstacles, being subdued by the strategies of Satan, we need spiritual light.

> In him was life; and the life was the light of men. And the light shineth in the darkness; and the darkness comprehended it not (John 1:4–5).

> Then spake Jesus again unto them, saying, I am the light of the world: he that followeth me shall not walk in darkness, but shall have the light of life (John 8:12).

We know that Jesus is the word made flesh, and all things were made by him, and without him was not anything made that was made (John 1:1–3).

What we need to understand is that the light God has given us day and night is Jesus or the word. The more of the word of God, the more of Jesus we have, and the more of Jesus means more light. The more light we have, the less we'll be tripped up in the darkness.

John 1:5 says the darkness comprehended it not. That means the darkness of evil has *never* been able to overcome, defeat, or conquer God's light. What that's revealing to God's soldier is that NOTHING is more powerful than God's light. No powers of darkness can extinguish it.

Since God promises to give us light day and night, why are God's soldiers stumbling in the darkness? Why are we losing the battle between the flesh and Spirit? Why are we making the wrong choices?

It's because we don't believe his word. If we did, we would be choosing to walk in the light of his word instead of allowing the darkness to trip us up. Israel saw the cloud by day and the fire by night and still they didn't believe. We have access to the word day and night. But how many read and study it? How many allow the word to transform how we think? How many use the light of the word when faced with the darkness of giants, storms, obstacles, or strategies of Satan? Whenever Jesus was faced with such, He used the light of the word (Matthew 4:1–11).

Do we believe the darkness and not the word? Is our light like a nightlight, a twenty-watt bulb, a hundred-watt bulb, or a flood light? The degree of our light is the degree of our recognizing and overcoming the darkness of evil.

Christ walked in the light of the noonday sun when facing the darkness. He has given us the word to do likewise. Let me explain. As I stated, the more of the word, the more of Jesus, and the more of Jesus means more light.

Jesus said whoever follows him shall not walk in darkness, but shall have the light of life. In other words, God's soldiers have the light of life. We have the word of God. Because we have Jesus, we have light to avoid the darkness.

We must comprehend when we are born again—delivered from the bondage of sin—we enter the wilderness like Israel. In the wilderness is where we decide to trust or not to trust God. Do we believe God will supply all our need of food, water, etc.? Or will we continuously murmur and complain?

In the previous chapter, I revealed that Jesus lived in the promises of God. We think the promises will eliminate any hard times. Although Christ's prayer was answered, the cup wasn't taken from him. However, He was given the grace to endure his Father's will.

As we face giants, storms, obstacles, we find out if we're a David who can face any giant. It's imperative for the storms, giants, etc. in our life. Without them, we'll never know who we really are in Christ. It's easy to tell others to be a David when they're facing a Goliath. But what are we when our Goliath (giant storm, giant obstacle, etc.) stands before us?

Will we be like the Israelites and forget the God who is present with us 24–7–365? Will we yield to the flesh because of the darkness trying to consume us? Will we be so filled with the light of Christ, that we take up our slingshot, *five* stones (trusting in God's grace), and destroy our Goliath?

In other words, will the flesh and Spirit conflict cause us to lose the inner battle of choice to unbelief, or will we win through faith? The flesh and Spirit conflict is won through denying self, remembering that God is always with us, trusting in God's grace that gives strength to replace our weakness, and believing that God will give us the ability to slay our giants.

Soldier of God, you are in the hands of the 24–7–365 God. He will always throw you a touchdown. He's already won, all you have to do is deny your flesh, choose to believe his word during the inner battle of choice, and allow him to make the calls!

Chapter 11

The Inner Battle of Choice

For the flesh lusteth against the Spirit, and the Spirit
against the flesh: and these are contrary the one to the
other: so that ye cannot do the things that ye would.

GALATIANS 5:17

FOR GOD'S SOLDIERS WHO have read through this book, this chapter
is meant to illuminate more clearly how to recognize and overcome
the flesh. By this time, we should comprehend that the inner battle
of choice rages during the flesh and Spirit conflict.

The spiritual conflict within God's soldiers involves our mind,
body, and spirit. This inner battle of choice determines whether
we'll yield to our sinful desires of the lust of the flesh, the lust of the
eyes, or the pride of life or surrender to the Spirit's commands. If we
give into our flesh, sin will control us.

Sin is ever lying at the door of our heart to influence our
choice. But if we relinquish our will to that of the Spirit, we'll continue under the authority and control of Christ. In other words, sin
will not rule us, but we'll rule over it (Genesis 4:7).

This battle field within each Christian of the conflict between flesh and Spirit will continue as long as we are on the earth. Because they are in opposition, our earthy life is one of constant conflict of choosing self or God, faith or unbelief, sin or righteousness. We must do warfare against our flesh daily in order to submit to God's will.

We don't win the battle one day and its victory is sure the next day. Let me reiterate what is said in chapter 1.

> And he said to them all, If any man will come after me, let him deny himself, and take up his cross daily, and follow me (Luke 9:23).

In the above Scripture, Jesus gave the secret or the key to self-deliverance. The only way for us to follow Jesus is to deny self on a daily basis. If we're indulging our flesh (self) we are not following Jesus. We can't claim to be a follower of Jesus Christ when we give into our flesh and obey it. We can only follow Jesus as we deny self or our fleshly desires and take up our cross daily.

It's a daily crucifying of self and its lusts. If we're going to reign with Jesus in the future, we must take up our cross daily, nail self to it, and follow Christ. We can't do this in our own power; we need the conquering power of the Holy Spirit in us to do this.

Through the guidance of and the conquering power of the Holy Spirit, God's soldiers will overcome the ungodly desires of our flesh and yield to the Spirit. We must not forget this battle will rage until we are with Jesus. Because God is a 24-7-365 God, we are NEVER left alone without the help we need to overcome. The Holy Spirit within gives the power to win the battle between the flesh and Spirit, by denying self, and making the choice to obey God's word.

> Now the works of the flesh are manifest, which are these: Adultery, fornication, uncleanness, lasciviousness, idolatry, witchcraft, hatred, variance, emulations, wrath, strife, seditions, heresies, envyings, murders, drunkenness, revellings, and such like: of the which I tell you before, as I have also told you in time past, that they which do such things shall not inherit the kingdom of God (Galatians 5:18–21).

Perhaps, many of us are not aware of how to recognize that we are in the flesh or have yielded to the flesh. We may say we aren't an adulterer or a murderer. But do we look at someone with lustful thoughts? Do we hate someone?

Jesus says, "Whosoever looketh on a woman to lust after her hath committed adultery with her already in his heart" (Matthew 5:28). This works both ways for men and women. If a woman looks with lust at a man, she has committed adultery in her heart. What thoughts go through our mind when looking at someone?

As for hate, Scripture says, "Whosoever hateth his brother is a murderer, and ye know that no murderer hath eternal life abiding in him" (I John 3:15). In other words, hate in our heart is being a murderer. Unless we repent by yielding to the Spirit and not the flesh when the flesh and Spirit conflict is raging, we will not win the inner battle of choice for God. Do we understand that having harsh feelings towards others is hate? Do we realize that hate makes us murderers in our heart?

We are born with a sinful nature with its corrupt desires, its resistance to God, and an insistence on going its own way. This took place in the garden where the first effects of choice happened. Because of Adam and Eve's disobedience, all mankind is now born with a nature opposite of God. Our sinful nature is the image of Satan. We again take on the nature of God when we're born again. However, that's when the flesh and Spirit conflict and the inner battle of choice becomes a reality.

Unless we are born again, we have no power over the lust of our flesh and have no inner power to resist its lust. Once the Holy Spirit takes up residence in us after the new birth, we now have the conquering power to overcome our sinful nature or our flesh and its propensity to sin.

Let me clarify some of the works of the flesh to help us identify when we have yielded to the flesh and not the Spirit. Unless we understand the seriousness of these sins, and the necessity of repentance, we'll not inherit the kingdom of God.

Fornication is sexual relations or sexual contact outside of a marriage relationship. It includes pornography that feeds sexual desires and sexually suggestive forms of entertainment, films, or writings. This is clearly seen in what the half-time has become in the Super Bowl. I enjoyed watching football, but NO longer watch it because of the evil communications it now propagates. It was a conflict between my flesh and Spirit and an inner battle to decide that I would NOT set any wicked thing before my eyes (Psalms 101:3).

Uncleanness is not only a reference to sexual sins, but evil behavior and ungodly traits and habits. It begins in secret thoughts and desires which lead to impurity affecting us morally and spiritually. This sin is revealed in what comes out of our mouth and our reactions. What comes out of our mouth, and how we react to situations, is what our heart is embracing.

Lasciviousness refers to improper behavior and a lack of self-control. This sin is revealed through those who follow inner passions and desires to the point of having no shame or thought for public decency. We see this sin flaunted in homosexuals who have no shame of their abomination to God. We see this sin flaunted in child rapists who have no shame of the destruction being inflicted on their victims. We see this sin flaunted in the abortionists who have no shame in murdering innocent children. The sad part is Christians are flaunting these sins through acceptance without shame and voting for those who are in favor of such perversion and immorality.

Idolatry includes worshiping spirits, false gods, persons, etc. instead of the true God. This sin is also seen whenever we love someone or something and give them status over obedience to God and his word. We must beware of putting more importance upon a person, place, or thing and ignore God's word. Let me explain. If God is prompting us to do something and a loved one advises against it, will we choose to obey God? Yes, that's a difficult stand, but who is our God? Do we worship the true and living God or do we idolize a person, place, or thing?

Wrath is explosive outbursts of anger resulting in violent words or actions. This sin is visualized when we allow anger to cause us to say hurtful things or physically harm those we disagree with. Do we become so angry at loved ones that we say cutting words to satisfy our flesh? Do we allow wrath to cause us to say angry words or do cruel actions because we were corrected, told we are in the flesh, or they disagree with our beliefs? Do we throw things, punch things, break things when angry? Wrath is where the flesh is controlling, we don't utilize self-control over our anger, and loose it as a breached dam.

Envying is being jealous or resentful in our dislike of others who have what we desire. It can be envious of their spouse, their children, their house, their job, their pet, their car, their position, their looks, etc. Do we envy others who have what we want? Do we envy others who have a better personality than us? Do we desire their position? What are we saying about others? Do we demean others because we are jealous, envious, or dislike them?

Unless we learn to recognize the works of the flesh in our life, we'll be ruled by its sinful desires. What we must comprehend is the sinful nature is firm and forceful. It's the natural habitation that we were born in. Why do we think the baby cries when it wants something? Why do we think the toddler will touch whatever told not to touch? Why do we think the young child will demand his/her rebellion against our rules? Why do we think the teenager insists he/she is an adult capable of making their own decisions that are opposite our set guidelines? Why do we think we yield to the flesh and not the Spirit?

All are the result of the sinful nature controlling us and not the Spirit. This truth must be grasped if we're to overcome our flesh. Anytime we allow our flesh to rule and not the Spirit, we are NO longer following Jesus, NO longer denying self, and NO longer taking up our cross. This is why the *devil wants to keep us ignorant or blind* in recognizing our flesh.

Our flesh will lead us to the broad and wide path that leads to destruction or Hell. If we are comfortable in our flesh or any sin, we have swerved from the straight and narrow path that leads to life or Heaven.

Let me give an example of how easily we yield to the flesh. We are asked a question and we lie. We know it was a lie, yet we ignore it because we felt justified in not telling the truth. Unless, we confess that we were in the flesh and not the Spirit, we have stepped into the wide path to destruction.

Instead of telling the lie, we should have refused to answer, told them it looked horrible, claimed it was not the person's business, etc. Yes, telling others it's not their business or the hat looks dreadful seems harsh. So, we lie instead of stating truth. What if Jesus didn't tell us that our sins separate us from God, and instead told us a lie, would we know truth?

Listen to me, I'm not saying that we'll always make the right choice. We have an old nature that's cunning and created in the image of Satan, and it will deceive us any time we stray from following Christ, the word of God, or truth. However, the key to overcoming the flesh and Spirit conflict and win the inner war or battle of choice is to recognize the flesh and its lusts.

Overcoming the inner battle of choice takes denying self what it wants. This warfare raging in us can be overwhelming. I mean, especially if we so desperately want to do something, crave something, or are tired of squeezing our flesh, and denying self what it desires.

Our example of self-denial is Jesus. He doesn't ask us to do anything that He didn't do. Chapter 9 reveals his inner battle of choice when in the clutches of his flesh and Spirit conflict. We'll never undergo the severity of his conflict. However, He revealed to us the necessity of recognizing the flesh when the conflict has the inner battle of choice raging. We see He yielded to the Spirit when He said, "Father, if thou be willing, remove this cup from me: nevertheless NOT my will, but thine, be done" (Luke 22:42).

Because He is a 24-7-365 God, He is able to replace the weakness of our flesh with the strength of his Spirit. This is accomplished as we recognize our flesh and its lust. In other words, it's time that God's soldiers take a good look at self (look in the mirror and see what sort of Christian we are). As we allow the Spirit to illuminate our words and actions and not center attention on the words and actions of others, the scales of self-blindness will fall. We seem to recognize that another has yielded to the flesh while being blind to our fleshly words and actions.

As soon as we realize that our words, our thoughts, or our actions are fleshly, we must confess that recognition. We must be willing to say we reacted in the flesh and not the Spirit. As we detect our fleshly words, our fleshly actions, and overcome their grasp, we are back on the straight and narrow path to denying self's rule in our life. Then whenever the flesh and Spirit conflict has the inner battle of choice raging, we'll follow Jesus and yield to the Spirit, deny self, and choose to obey God's word!